TO HEAVEN WITH DIANA!

ALSO BY GERALD VANN, O.P.

On Being Human
Morals Makyth Man
Morality and War
Of His Fullness
St. Thomas Aquinas
The Heart of Man
The Divine Pity
His Will is our Peace
Eve and the Gryphon
The Pain of Christ
Awake in Heaven
The Two Trees
The Seven Swords
The High Green Hill
The Water and the Fire
The Paradise Tree
The Son's Course

IN COLLABORATION WITH P.K. MEAGHER, O.P.

The Temptations of Christ

TO HEAVEN WITH DIANA!

A Study of
Jordan of Saxony and Diana d'Andalò
with a translation of the
Letters of Jordan
by
GERALD VANN, O.P.

iUniverse, Inc.
New York   Lincoln   Shanghai

To Heaven With Diana!
A Study of Jordan of Saxony and Diana d'Andalò with a Translation of the Letters of Jordan

iUniverse books may be ordered through booksellers or by contacting:

iUniverse
2021 Pine Lake Road, Suite 100
Lincoln, NE 68512
www.iuniverse.com
1-800-Authors (1-800-288-4677)

First Edition © Gerald Vann, O.P., 1960
Published by Pantheon Books, Inc., New York.

Reprinted with permission of
the English Province of the Order of Preachers.

ISBN-13: 978-0-595-38586-7 (pbk)
ISBN-13: 978-0-595-82967-5 (ebk)
ISBN-10: 0-595-38586-9 (pbk)
ISBN-10: 0-595-82967-8 (ebk)

Printed in the United States of America

On the occasion of the
Eighth Centenary of the Foundation of
The Nuns of the Order of Preachers
at Prouilhe, France
(1206–2006)
The Dominican Nuns
of the
Monastery of Our Lady of the Rosary
Summit, New Jersey
dedicate this book to
The Dominican Nuns
Past, Present, and Future
Firstborn Daughters of St. Dominic
Sisters of Jordan and his beloved Diana

You are so deeply engraven in my heart that the more I realize how truly you love me from the depths of your soul, the more incapable I am of forgetting you and the more constantly you are in my thoughts; for your love of me moves me profoundly, and makes my love for you burn more strongly...

—*Jordan of Saxony to Diana d'Andalò*
Letter 25

NIHIL OBSTAT
RAULPHUS HODSOLL, O.P., S.T.L.
GERARDUS MEATH, O.P., M.A.
IMPRIMI POTEST
HENRICUS ST. JOHN, O.P.
PRIOR PROVINCIALIS
LONDINI DIE 20 APRILIS 1959
NIHIL OBSTAT
GERARDUS CULKIN, L.S.H.
CENSOR DEPUTATUS
IMPRIMATUR
✠JACOBUS
EPISCOPUS HAGULSTADENSIS
ET NOVOCASTRENSIS
NOVOCASTRI DIE 24 APRILIS 1959

CONTENTS

FOREWORD TO THE SECOND EDITION

Some may wonder whether it is prudent to publish today the private letters of a Dominican Master of the Order, who would address his correspondent with the words, *carissima mea*. That which is true, however, should never be feared. These letters that are a pearl of Dominican spirituality, together with the magnificent introduction of the late Gerald Vann, O.P., show how it is possible for divine charity to transform human hearts with a warm and fraternal love. If religious life were not to change hearts of stone into hearts of flesh, what would be its value? We have taken up the adventure of the Lord's call so as to love more and not less, and so as to have the abundant life that the Lord has promised us. Consecrated life can only be a valid proposition and a way of life if it is lived out within a true faith and true divine and human charity.

St. Dominic Guzman began the founding of the Dominican Order exactly 800 years ago by establishing a community of Dominican nuns in Prouilhe, in the South of France. Most of the sisters were converts from a Manichean heresy that denied the value of the body and of marriage. By setting up a community of nuns, whose life was centered on Jesus Christ, Dominic affirmed the goodness of creation, of humanity, of love. His gaiety and fraternal friendship with men and women of his Order showed the way for a joyful Christianity capable of fulfilling the hunger of the human heart. He knew that the mission of preaching the saving Word in which men and women of his Order were to be engaged could only profit from complementary shared experiences, from mutual support and common contemplative prayer. His immediate successor, blessed Jordan of Saxony, who was instrumental in eliciting the vocations of thousands of men to the Order, had received the grace of being supported by the friendship and prayers of the loving heart of blessed Diana, a nun of the Monastery of St. Agnes in Bologna. His letters to Diana (Diana's letters to Jordan have not survived—maybe because men are not so attentive in collecting personal documentation!) manifest the supernatural quality of their love. Jordan's attentiveness and concern is humane. His love and support is practical. His spiritual guidance always protects Diana against excesses of asceticism that often perplex the minds of religious. His gratitude for the response of Diana is profound. And all along the focus of his love for Diana is lived out within a simultaneous and deeper focus on God himself. As a psalm refrain, his letters repeat: "My eyes are ever towards the Lord." It is the love for Jesus that brought them together, and it is echoes of that divine love, resplendent in their hearts that granted their love its depth, purity and stability. The quality of that divine love was tested by their obedience to the will of God. Diana persevered in her convent in Bologna, seeing Jordan only occasionally, as he would visit her community. Jordan travelled around Europe (mainly on foot!) serving the Order as its Master, up to his shipwreck and death off the coast of the Holy Land.

Within the entire Dominican Family we celebrate in 2006 the 800th anniversary of the founding of the first community of Dominican nuns. May this little book help us to perceive the importance of the contemplative dimension of our lives and its liberating influence on our hearts!

FR. CARLOS A. AZPIROZ COSTA, O.P.
Master of the Order of Preachers

Rome, Santa Sabina, Christmas 2005

FOREWORD TO THE FIRST EDITION

This study of the letters of Jordan of Saxony to Diana d'Andalò, which were written between 1222 and 1237, is not meant to be either an exercise in paleography or an historical monograph on the period. Its purpose is simple: to reveal through them first the personalities of the two people concerned; secondly, the quality of their friendship; thirdly, the substance of Jordan's teaching as a wise director of souls.

The translation has been made from the Latin text in the edition of Dr. Berthold Altaner: *Die Briefe Jordans von Sachsen*, in the series *Quellen und Forschungen zur Geschichte des Dominikanerordens in Deutschland* edited by Paulus von Loë (Leipzig, 1925). A more recent edition of the text has been made by P. A. Walz, O.P.: *Beati Jordani de Saxonia Epistulae* (Rome, 1951). The French translation made by Marguerite Aron: *Bienheureux Jourdain de Saxe: Lettres à la B. Diane d'Andalò* (Desclée, De Brouwer, Lille-Bruges, 1924) has been consulted throughout, though not always followed. Both these works, and also Aron's life of Jordan, have been invaluable for the writing of the *Introduction* and the plotting of Jordan's many journeys. If the present translation sends English readers back to these and other sources for fuller information both about the two people concerned and about Jordan's teaching it will have served its purpose.

GERALD VANN, O.P.

EDITOR'S ACKNOWLEDGEMENTS

One of the first lessons a Dominican novice learns is the importance of community life, that "oneness in mind and heart"[1] which is the steady heartbeat of the "Holy Preaching." It is what gives our Order its universality and its unity. From the beginnings of this project, I have experienced that "oneness" through the support of my sisters and brothers in St. Dominic. Whether expressed in interest or intercession, word or deed, their engagement and collaboration in bringing Gerald Vann's Dominican classic back into print gave the undertaking a marvelous momentum. "Behold! how good and pleasant it is when brothers (*and sisters!*) dwell in unity."[2]

My deep gratitude extends to all the "sharers in the work":[3] my prioress, Sr. Mary Martin Jacobs, O.P., who welcomed our monastery's sponsorship of the project; Fr. Allan White, O.P., provincial of the English Dominican Province (Blackfriars) who graciously gave us the all-important permission to reprint the book; reviewers Fr. Timothy Radcliffe, O.P., Fr. Paul Murray, O.P., Sr. Claire Marie Rolf, O.P., and Sr. Mary John Molesworth, O.P., who responded so readily and so eloquently; Fr. Carlos A. Azpiroz Costa, O.P., Master of the Order, who, in the midst of his commitments, found the time to write more than a "little word" on the book in his superb foreward; Fr. Manuel Merten, O.P., Promoter of the Nuns, who showed this project the same warm solicitude he shows to the nuns; Fr. Juan-Diego Brunetta, O.P. for his editorial assistance; and Fr. John Paul Walker, O.P., for his constant encouragement.

Non-Dominicans also figure prominently in this work: Jim Manney of Loyola Press who came to my rescue in providing reprint permission advice; iUniverse's Michael Fiedler, publishing consultant, and publishing services associates Mindy Peck and Kerry Mickle, who showed this former editorial assistant an uncharacteristic professionalism and patience, and won her respect and gratitude.

---

[1] *Rule of Augustine,* chap. 1.   [2] *Ps* 133, 1 RSV.   [3] *Letter 14.*

And, lastly, I wish to thank Bl. Jordan of Saxony and Bl. Diana d'Andalò, whose intercession was felt throughout.

SR. JUDITH MIRYAM BONESKI, O.P.
Editor

Summit, New Jersey, January 18, 2006
Feast of St. Margaret of Hungary, O.P.

PART I

Jordan and Diana

THE cavalcade rattled angrily through the cobbled streets and out of the city—*concursus ingens populorum,* says the primitive chronicle, a huge assembly of people, men and women, relatives and friends—and galloped through the slanting rays of the reddening sun for Ronzano. These men, Andreolo and his six sons, were not to be trifled with: a powerful, impetuous, warrior race; accustomed to command, and to exact obedience, it was a new and unpleasant experience for them to be defied by a girl of eighteen. Andreolo himself was a *pretore delta montagna* or *podestà,* mayor, of the mountain territories of Bologna; he had troops under his command. His eldest son, Brancaleone, was *podestà* of Genoa and perhaps a senator of Rome; another son, Castellano, was *podestà* of Modena and seems likewise to have become a senator of Rome; Lodrenzo, the youngest, was so successful in reconciling the warring factions in Bologna that he was called to be *podestà* of various cities and eventually of Florence; his attempt there to keep the peace between Guelphs and Ghibellines caused him to be accused of favouring the former and earned him the enmity of Dante who consigned him to the Inferno. He was moreover the founder and first prior of the Frati Gaudenti, the knightly and religious confraternity called officially the Congregation of the Glorious Virgin.

They had been defied, tricked, by a girl; they galloped off at once to Ronzano to reassert their authority, if necessary by force. Imagine an escarpment on one of the last bastions of the Apennines; Bologna is spread out beneath it, to the west the eye sweeps to the Adriatic, to the north you see the towering peaks of the Alps. On the plateau there is a convent of canonesses of St. Augustine; for the Bolognese it was a place of pilgrimage; it was also a favourite spot for excursions because of the beauty of the view. But Andreolo and his sons were in no mood for pious pilgrimages or pretty views. Their only concern was to give the nuns a good lesson and to speak their mind to Diana.

It was the 22 July, 1220 or 1221. The trouble had started two or three years earlier than that. These were the years when St. Dominic was laying the foundations of his Order of Preachers; his plan was to set up houses of the Order in the university cities; in 1218, there being

3

already priories in Toulouse, Paris, Madrid and Rome, he decided on a foundation in Bologna, which was one of the leading European centres of learning. The friars made a very modest beginning, in a little house and church near the schools of law. But they were invited by the canons regular to preach in the church of Santa Maria in Mascarella, which was near the d'Andalò house; and Diana, who was attracted by the things of the mind, went to hear them.

Of her childhood we know nothing; but we know a good deal about her as she was when she first came into contact with the friars. She was of outstanding beauty: *decora facie et venusto aspectu,* says the contemporary chronicle, lovely of face and charming to behold; there exists a portrait of her, reproduced by the Bollandists,[1] which they thought to have been painted either shortly after her death or while she was still alive; its authenticity was vouched for by the Count Valerius de Zanis, who saw it done. Her contemporaries also speak of her as eloquent and learned; and there is no doubt about her charm, her high spirits, her courage, and that faculty of making swift and sure decisions which, as one of her modern biographers remarks, is often found in women who have been brought up in the society of men. She was full of the joy of living; full too of the joy of her own beauty and the power it gave her. Then, in 1218, the distinguished Dominican, Reginald of Orléans, came to Bologna.

Reginald's preaching, here as elsewhere, had astonishing power, and astonishing results: a new Elias, Jordan of Saxony was to call him; the whole city was stirred. The first effect of his coming was to bring recruits from among the doctors of the university; then, one day, Diana came to listen to him, and his text was taken from words of St. Peter and St. Paul about luxury in dress. Diana had no doubt come out of curiosity; but his attack on worldliness had a profound effect on her: with characteristic decision she went forthwith and confessed to him, and threw off at once and for all what she now saw to be the tyranny of the world of fashion and superficiality. There followed a complete change in her way of life. Under Reginald's guidance she remained in her father's house, she continued to wear the rich clothes proper to her

---

[1] [Association of ecclesiastical scholars who compiled the monumental *Acta Sanctorum* (*Lives of the Saints*), an hagiographical encyclopedia, the publication of which spanned several centuries (1643–1940). The name "Bollandists" is derived from the name of its first editor, Jean Bolland, S.J. (1596–1665). *Ed.*]

position, she shared her life as before with her family and her friends; but beneath the silk and jewels of which the chronicle speaks she wore a hairshirt and an iron chain, and in order to have time for prayer she rose early every morning and stayed alone in her room till the hour of Tierce.[2] Moreover she made a public act of self-consecration to God in the church of St. Nicholas, Reginald and others being present; and in 1219 St. Dominic, who had recalled Reginald to Paris and himself replaced him in Bologna, received her vow of virginity and her promise to become a religious as soon as she should be free to do so.

But to a mind as forthright as hers this sort of compromise soon became very irksome, the more so as under her influence some of her friends had begun to follow her example. To St. Dominic she confided her desire to build a convent where they could lead fully the life of Dominican contemplatives. Her family, she said, would surely provide the money. St. Dominic thought and prayed about the project; then he made up his mind, and his decision was a remarkable one. The friars had had to look for more spacious quarters in the city and had in this respect been fortunate: Rodolpho di Faenza, the rector of the Church of St. Nicholas of the Vineyards, joined their ranks and with the bishop's permission his church was made over to them while the adjoining land belonging to the d'Andalò family was eventually, after a good deal of coaxing by Diana, given them by Peter her grandfather. Here, close to the schools of law, they found themselves really a part of the life of the university, their house a centre of intellectual activity, their numbers rapidly increasing. But they had to build; and it was while the building was in progress that Diana suggested her plan to St. Dominic. His decision was that her convent should be begun, even though it meant that St. Nicholas' had to remain unfinished.

The decision is startling until one has realized the role of the Second Order, the monasteries of contemplative nuns, in St. Dominic's total plan. The motto of the Order is *veritas,* truth: the work of the friars is to teach the truth, and the truth is not easily come by. The truth is God; and to teach the truth as it should be taught one must learn God: one must be not only a student, learning about God through the rational disciplines of philosophy and theology, but also a contemplative, learn-

---

[2] [The third hour after sunrise, when the liturgical office of the same name was prayed. *Ed.*]

ing God through intuitive awareness and above all through prayer. So the aim of the Order is expressed in the beginning of the Dominican Constitutions: *contemplata aliis tradere,* to pass on to others the fruit of contemplation. In St. Dominic's scheme the friars were meant to be busy men, to undertake the work of teaching or preaching in its various forms; yet all their work would necessarily be shallow and therefore in the long run perhaps do more harm than good unless behind it there was the light and the power of contemplation. The practical difficulty is obvious: if they are to be so active how will they find the time to be contemplatives?

The answer lies in the organic unity of the Church, Christ's Mystical Body: the light and the power necessary to supplement their own attempts—perhaps even, where necessary, to make good their failure—to be men of prayer should be provided for them by their religious sisters. As Adam needed and was given a helpmeet like to himself, so—the analogy is Père Cormier's[3]—the first Order needed and was given a helpmeet to share its work and its life, and a helpmeet like to itself because stamped with the same family spirit, the spirit of Dominic. The monasteries would be the Order's centres of energy; at all costs therefore they must be provided.

This essential necessity of contemplation for the life of action, for the life of society as a whole, is often not understood nowadays. Goodwill, zeal, energy are not enough: misguided benevolence may do as much harm in the long run as sheer wickedness. Action without contemplation is blind. So it is part of the traditional economy of the Church's life that there should be some who give themselves wholly and exclusively to the contemplative life precisely in order that the activity of others may be guided and empowered and fruitful. St. Dominic knew when he founded his Order that the men who followed him would, if they were faithful to their calling, have an immense amount of work to do; they were to try to be contemplative themselves, but even if they were truly zealous, all but the greatest and holiest of them would find the time factor against them: they would not gain from their own prayer alone the

---

3 [Hyacinthe-Marie Cormier (1832–1916), 76th Master General of the Order of Preachers. Known as an artisan of peace, he guided the Order through the difficult time of Modernism. He was beatified by Pope John Paul II in 1994. His feast is kept on May 21. *Ed.*]

power that their work would need. So before the work was started at all he had founded his convent of purely contemplative nuns; it was they who were to empower their brethren; it was they who were to bring down upon the work of the Order the blessing, the wisdom and love and energy, of God.

It is this social aspect of the contemplative life that is so often misunderstood. People think of contemplative monks and nuns as leaving the world to fend for itself and retiring to a safe retreat to look after their own souls. But every Christian comes to God *per Christum,* through and in Christ; and to share the life of Christ is to share the love and the labours of Christ. As the Church is indivisible, so its work is indivisible: we have different gifts to bring to the common task, different functions to fulfil, but we act as members of the single indivisible Body of Christ; those whose life is prayer find their prayer expressed and fulfilled in the labours of the vineyard, and those who labour draw on the power gen erated by the hidden life of prayer. The story of the nun in Benson's[4] *Light Invisible* puts this very clearly: "I perceived that this black figure knelt at the centre of reality and force, and with the movements of her will and lips controlled spiritual destinies for eternity. There ran out from this peaceful chapel lines of spiritual power that lost themselves in the distance, bewildering in their profusion and terrible in the intensity of their hidden fire.... Yes, and I in my arrogance had thought that my life was more active in the world than hers."

St. Dominic took his decision. He himself had to leave for Rome; but he left the work in charge of his sons. Immediately, however, they found their way blocked: there was trouble with the bishop over the proposed site, above all there was trouble with the d'Andalò family, who roughly refused the money. It is possible and indeed likely that the violence of their opposition to the idea that Diana should become a nun was due to the fact that they had an advantageous marriage in mind for her: the rich Torelli family, into which Lodrenzo had married, is mentioned in that connection. At any rate they stood firm. Diana for her part refused to be discouraged: if she could not be a Dominican she would be some other kind of nun; she made her plans with characteris-

---

4 [Msgr. Robert Hugh Benson (1871–1914), English author and Anglican priest who converted to Roman Catholicism in 1903. His most famous book is his apocalyptic novel, *Lord of the World* (1907). *Ed.*]

tic boldness and decision. It was no use arguing indefinitely; the thing was to act. So we come back to 22 July 1221.

She organized an excursion with her friends; and what pleasanter objective could there be on a July day than Ronzano? They arrived with a large escort at the convent. But then, to the consternation of her friends, she disappeared into the convent; she besought the nuns to admit her to their company; she pleaded to such effect that in the end they gave her their habit there and then. The party hurried back to tell her family what she had done; they were furious and rode out to bring her back. There ensued an undignified scene, half tragedy, half comedy. The family forced its way into the convent; Diana refused to leave, implored, resisted; they dragged her out by main force, so roughly indeed that one of her ribs was broken.

For a long time she was laid up, unable to move—she was never completely cured—but her physical pain was less of a trial to her than the fact that her family kept her a close prisoner, guarded day and night and denied all communication with the outside world. St. Dominic returned to Bologna, and managed to send her letters of encouragement; but she was soon bereft of that consolation, for on 6 August—only fifteen days after the Ronzano episode if we put it in 1221—he died. Still Diana refused to be daunted; and as soon as she could get about again she fled again to Ronzano. There was no knowing what the family might have done at this second defiance; Diana was certainly not lacking in bravery. As it happened they did nothing; they left her in peace. But her heart was far from being at peace; she wanted to be a Dominican, and her dream seemed as far from realization as ever. Then Jordan of Saxony came to Bologna; and a new chapter in her life began.

There is one adjective in particular which all who knew Jordan and wrote of him seem to regard as peculiarly fitting to his character so that it becomes indissolubly linked with his name: it is *dulcis,* gentle, sweet-natured. He was a man of manifold gifts; but his sweetness and charm seemed to colour all his other gifts, and to be the secret of his amazing success in his work for souls.

In the *Lives of the Brethren,* the thirteenth-century collection of legends and stories of the primitive days of the Order of Preachers edited by Gérard de Frachet, these qualities are very apparent. There he is spoken of as "beloved of God and man"; "his tender pity" we are told, "was always awakened at the sight of misery and distress"; "so kind and gentle was he towards his own brethren...he tried to correct faults more by winning gentleness and trusting his subjects than by harsh discipline, although he knew how to use this means as well but always having regard to time and place and persons"; "whenever he came to a convent he would first of all get the blessing and salute his brethren, then he would go to the bedside of the sick and cheer them, after which if there were novices in the house he would gather them round him and talk familiarly with them, and if any were downcast or beset with temptations he would very soon gladden them."

It was not only human beings that were charmed by him: "his words bore weight not only with men but even with the animals"; one day when some of the brethren were walking in a lane outside Lausanne an ermine ran across their path and, frightened by their cries, scurried off into a cave; when Jordan, who had been walking behind with another friend, came up to them they told him of the "beautiful snow-white animal" they had seen and of how they wished he too had seen it; whereupon Jordan went to the mouth of the cave and bade the animal come out that he might admire it; the ermine at once obeyed, "and standing quietly in front of the cave looked up into his face. Then putting one hand under its front paws, he fondly stroked its head and back with the other," and then, blessing it, told it to go back to its lair, and "the animal then darted back into the cave."[5]

Of Jordan's brilliance the mere facts of his meteoric career leave us in no doubt: coming of a noble family of Westphalia, first studying and then lecturing as a Master in the University of Paris, he had hardly entered the Order of Preachers when he was appointed by St. Dominic to be the first prior provincial of Lombardy and a year later, on St. Dominic's death, he was unanimously elected Master General; on terms of familiarity with popes and princes, even the redoubtable Emperor,[6] he was at the same time able, as he himself said,[7] to "become

---

[5] "The Legend of Blessed Jordan of Saxony, Second Master General of the Order of Preachers," Part IV, chaps. 3, 1, 4, 8 in *Lives of the Brethren of the Order of Preachers, 1206–1259 (Vitae Fratrum)*, translated by Placid Conway, O.P.; edited by Bede Jarrett, O.P. (London: Blackfriars Publications, 1955).

[6] [Frederick II (1194–1250). *Ed.*]   [7] *Lives*, Part IV, chap. 31.

9

all things to all men"; "he is reckoned to have drawn over a thousand subjects to the Order";[8] the appeal of his charm was universal.

His letters too reveal the humanist, the man of culture and erudition, the theologian, the biblical scholar, the wise and shrewd director of souls; they also reveal a writer who is something of a poet, who can express his wisdom and erudition in a style which has been described as "rare and more than rare, unique, in the Middle Ages":[9] the wisdom always *dulcis,* the erudition made feather-light by the magic of his charm.

The same lightness of touch is apparent in his wit and humour. In the *Lives of the Brethren* there is the engaging story of the Saxon nobleman who stole a cow belonging to Master Jordan's mother (why he should have behaved so oddly is not explained) and whose son shortly after entered the Order, whereupon "the friends and retainers came to complain of this" to Jordan, and "chided him sharply for having taken away their master's son"; but he reminded them of the good old Saxon custom "that when any wrong has been done to a woman no one deems it unfair for her son to avenge the injury," and to this they "all nodded their assent. "Well," said he, "since your master injured my mother by robbing her of her cow, what wrong have I done him, think you, in walking off with his calf?"[10]

Another anecdote from the same source is relevant here because of the reference in *Letter 15* to the fact that being in Trent he was able to preach to the people, that being a German-speaking region. He did not allow barriers of language to be insurmountable. Once when he was "beyond the seas" he was asked by some Knights Templars from France to preach to them: "and this is the simple way in which he got over the difficulty. Wishing them to understand from the outset that he knew but little French, and trusting, by means of an occasional word in that tongue, they might gather the meaning of a long sentence in German, he stood with his back to a wall of about his own height, and began: "Brethren, supposing an ass were standing on the other side of this wall, and were simply to raise his head high enough for you to see one of his big ears, we should all conclude rightly that a whole ass was there, for so we would take in the whole by means of a part."[11]

The two friars who wrote to the community at Paris to break the news of Jordan's death referred to him as "our sweet Father and

---

[8] *Lives,* Part IV, chap. 3.   [9] Aron, Introduction to *Lettres,* p. xv.
[10] *Lives,* Part IV, chap. 31.   [11] *Lives,* Part IV, chap. 31.

Master."[12] So he had always been known, universally: *dulcis pater;* and when, reading Diana's story, we meet him for the first time in Bologna it is his charm and sweetness which are immediately evident, and which in fact solved at once as though at the touch of a wand what had seemed till then to be an insoluble problem.

The houses of the Order had by then been grouped into provinces, of which Lombardy was one; and Jordan was the provincial of Lombardy. When he arrived at Bologna soon after the death of St. Dominic, Diana sought him out and told him of her adventures and dreams, the dreams that Dominic had shared. From that day forward they were never to be far from each other's thoughts; of that the letters which have come down to us are sufficient evidence. It is a tragedy that none of Diana's letters to Jordan have been preserved; but we have the fifty that he wrote to her or to what was soon to be her community—thirty-seven of them are addressed to Diana herself—and their vivid, richly allusive Latin reveals to us not only his own heart but hers. His first concern was to reconcile Diana and her family; he went to see them, he talked to them; and under the influence of his gentleness and his charm their hostility melted away, their opposition was at an end. The difficulty with the bishop was solved by the proposal of another site; a *domuncula parva,* a tiny little house, was built; and there at last Diana, with four other Bolognese ladies, was installed, and her Dominican life began.

That was not until June 1223. In May of the previous year Jordan had to go to Paris to attend a General Chapter[13] of the Order, and there he had been elected Master General—the head of the whole Order. It

---

[12] Cf. *infra*, p. 102.

[13] [Juan-Diego Brunetta, O.P., offers a comprehensive yet succinct definition of the Dominican chapter: "The chapter-system rose out of the monastic model of governance. The professed members of the monastery comprised the chapter which was the organ for exhortations by the abbot as well as the handling of the business of the monastery that required input from all the members (e.g., the acceptance of new members or voting for a new abbot). This system was adopted by the canons (chapters used by bishops to help govern dioceses), and later by Dominic for his new order. In the Dominican context, a general chapter represents the friars throughout the world and is the highest authority of the order; the master of the order serves as the executor of the decrees of the general chapter." ("The Canonical Status of Persons, Structures, and Relationships in the Order of Preachers: An Historical-Juridical Study," [J.C.D. diss., The Catholic University of America, 2003], p. 16, n. 1), *Ed.*]

was as Master General that he returned to Bologna for the opening of the convent. In the meantime Diana had remained at Ronzano; and it was while she was there that he sent her the first of the letters that have come down to us.

It is impossible to capture and hold in English the full fragrance of Jordan's Latin: warmth and grace, humanity and mystical ardour are all alike expressed in a prose of which almost every phrase is an echo, immediate or remote, of the Bible or the breviary: it is clear that Jordan was so steeped in the Scriptures that his thought naturally clothed itself in its language and imagery; his sentences are a tapestry woven of these diverse and richly evocative threads, sometimes inserted in their own original significance, sometimes applied to fresh material so that a new significance is superimposed upon the old sometimes only half expressed, like an echo that comes faintly, in snatches, to the ear; but always and effortlessly giving an impression of depth upon depth, like a landscape in which mountain ranges run parallel, back and back, till at last they are swallowed up in the distant sky.[14]

The probable date of this first letter is Advent, 1222; Diana is not yet a Dominican, and cannot therefore be addressed technically as a sister by Jordan; but the formality of the opening is quickly warmed and freshened and made deeply personal; in the passage about hills and plains and strongholds there is an obvious reference to the heights of Ronzano, where Diana was still waiting with all the patience she could muster for the fulfilment of her dream.

"To the Lady Diana, his daughter in loving awe of the Father, his sister by adoption in the Son, his beloved in the love of the Spirit, his companion in the religious life: Brother Jordan, useless servant of the Order of Preachers: health, a swift deliverance from present sorrows, and enjoyment of the joys that are to come.

"It was the greatness of your desire which impelled you to write the letter you sent me: let me then tell you a little about the cause of that heavenly desire. Dearest sister, the longing of the patriarchs of old invited Christ, your Bridegroom, God's Son, to suffering: and he came. How then should he not come when your longing invites him to joy? Therefore let all your longing be fixed on heaven. He who would not

---

[14] The references are omitted in the short extracts from the letters given here in this *Introduction*, but will be found in the text which follows.

be bound in hell must bind himself to heavenly things: he who dwells in the plains knows no safety for he is exposed to the attacks of every enemy, but he who is encamped behind the walls and towers of a fortified city, he is secure. You then, beloved, do not pitch your tent in the plains; but as David fled from the face of Saul to the stronghold of Maspha, do you also dwell in desire in the heavenly strongholds.

"You do not know German, I think: for indeed you have never been in that country. Those who are of this world speak only the language of this world, for he that is of the earth, of the earth he speaketh. You then, beloved, if you would learn the language of heaven must dwell in heaven by desire: then, when you come back, and read in books or hear from preachers about the things of the spirit, you will understand what they say: for to understand the tongues of the angels you must live in the land of the angels.

"There are in man, as you know, two elements, body and soul; and the body is for ever seeking to satisfy its needs in the realm of material things lest it die of hunger: but the soul is more important than the body: do not then, beloved, be less concerned for the soul, but on the contrary send it forth sometimes to seek its food in the land of the spirit, that food which is not to be found in the earth and which is bought not with silver but with loving desire.

"Who would be so foolish as to allow himself to die for lack of a food which he could have simply by desiring it? Say then with the psalmist: My eyes are ever towards the Lord, like the eyes of a poor man looking longingly for an alms from the rich. The bees gather earth's honey from earth's flowers, and, careful for their future needs, garner it in their hives: your spirit must die unless it is fed with heavenly honey, for I know that it is of delicate temper and will disdain the nourishment of coarser foods. Send forth your spirit, therefore, beloved, to the flowers of heaven's fields which never fade, that it may draw honey from them and live; and set aside part of what it gathers in the hive of your heart that if sometimes its desires should languish it may find within itself, in these reserves, a renewal of delight. But you, beloved, when all these desires are fulfilled in you, do not forget the poor man who writes you this letter."[15]

---

[15] *Letter 1.*

"My eyes are ever towards the Lord": in all the advice which Jordan was to give Diana this thought is always present. He was to lead her to perfect love and to the peace of soul and the joy that come of perfect love: but this is the only way, to keep one's eye on the Lord and not on oneself. He was to help her to meet misfortune without dismay, to be temperate in her austerities, to be fearless, to love humility and poverty: always it was the same essential lesson, "My eyes are ever towards the Lord."

There was to be ample opportunity for her to perfect her joy and her fortitude; there were to be many trials and many sorrows. But she could never be alone in them: always Jordan was at hand to comfort and strengthen her, either by his presence or more frequently by his letters. Four sisters were brought from the now well-established convent of St. Sixtus at Rome that the new recruits might learn from them the rule and spirit of the Order; and one of these, Cecilia, was made prioress, so that Diana was not in a position of authority. But she was, in Cormier's phrase, *l'âme de tout,* the heart of the community; and it was to her that Jordan wrote, not only to help and console her in her own particular troubles, but that through her he might help the community in their common difficulties.

The first burden they had to shoulder was that of grinding poverty. It was part of Dominic's ideal that they should live a frugal life; but the terrible indigence of their early years was a different matter, and it was not relieved until 1230 when they were at last given the revenues of the convent of St. Adalbert. Jordan's letters in these years reflect a concern which may well have had their temporal needs especially in mind. In the summer of 1223 he writes: "To Diana his beloved sister in Christ, brother Jordan, unprofitable servant of the Order of Preachers: eternal health…. I beg you, of your charity in the Lord, let not your heart be troubled nor let it be afraid if you must suffer tribulation for Christ's sake; for if we are partakers of his sufferings, so shall we be also of his consolations. But let your service of God be a reasonable service, that you may please your invisible Bridegroom. Be strengthened in the Lord: whatever burden he may lay upon you, accept it, and in sorrow be strong to endure and find patience in your lowliness. The Lord be with you."[16]

[16] *Letter 5.*

14

The next letter concerns a different kind of trial, but one which weighed heavily on Diana's heart. Jordan's health was delicate and his labours and journeyings were immense: always so gentle with others, he was ruthless to himself, and during his long absences Diana was always anxious. "Since I cannot see you, as I would and as you would, with my bodily eyes," he tells her, "I have written to you a number of times since I left Bologna lest hearing various vague rumours about me you should be troubled in mind. You must know then that at Brescia I was stricken with fever but by the grace of God I recovered my strength and came on to Milan, and I hope in the Lord Jesus that I shall be able to continue my journey. Be consoled therefore in the Lord, that I thereby may be consoled also, for your consolation is a joy and gladness to me before God."[17]

Again he writes from Paris in the spring of 1224, reassuring her about his health, telling her, as he loved to do, about his successes for the Order, inspiring her with the thought of the joys that await the true lovers of God. "Since my arrival in Paris I have been almost all the time in good health except that in the middle of Lent I had a slight attack of tertian fever.[18] As for the scholars at the university, by God's grace things have gone well enough: between Advent and Easter about forty novices joined the Order, of whom many are Masters, others are well-lettered, and of many others again we have high hopes. Thank God then for the ones we have received, and pray for those whom we still need and hope to receive, that he may work in them both to will and to accomplish, according to his good will. For yourself, and for your daughters and mine, see to it (as indeed I hope you are doing) that you are all firm in patience, rooted in humility, enlarged in love; and strive always to grow in every virtue that you may go from strength to strength until the Lord of Lords is revealed in Sion, in that eternal and abiding Jerusalem where we shall see him as he is, and seeing be filled with unutterable joy, a joy no man can take from us."[19]

In January or February of the next year, 1225, Jordan wrote again, this time to the community of St. Agnes as a whole; and his letter is like

---

[17] *Letter 6.*

[18] [A fever, especially a malarial fever, with symptoms that appear every other day. *Ed.*]

[19] *Letter 9.*

a compendium of the teaching he gave them through the years with its gentle prudence and lofty idealism, its gaiety and its strength, its recurrent underlying motif, "My eyes are ever towards the Lord." It begins with a clear statement of what, following St. Dominic, he conceived the role of the contemplative sisters to be in relation to the friars: "For the moment I write to you only briefly, for I hope by God's gift to be able very soon to talk with you. But meanwhile, beloved daughters, do you each and all in your prayers to God beg him to give me his good grace, unhappy sinner that I am, that in the might of that grace prevenient and supporting I may be able to carry out all his will in the ministry he has entrusted to me. For I have great trust in your prayers, especially when you all invoke him with one mind and one heart, for it can hardly be that where many pray together some should not be heard.

"If any unwonted temptations come upon you, do not be affrighted: these are the wars and seditions against which the Lord would have his servants and handmaids to be strong and great of heart, since he himself, whose battle you fight, is your helper. For indeed what prince, seeing his tender little handmaidens or his own sisters fighting against a cruel enemy because of him and on his behalf would not at once arise, especially if he himself were mighty in battle, provided they did not take to flight at the time of attack but turned to entreat the face of their lord. Fight therefore not only manfully but prudently; for as Solomon tells us, war is managed with due ordering, and you will fight with prudence if you set out to subdue your carnal nature not precipitately but little by little, advancing by measured steps in the way of the virtues, not trying to fly but climbing cautiously up the scale of perfection till at length you come to the summit of all perfection. And, briefly to conclude: in all things you should observe due measure...for only the love of God knows neither measure nor moderation. And that love is nourished, not by the afflicting of the flesh but by holy desires and loving contemplation and through the cherishing of that sisterly love whereby each of you loves the others as herself."[20]

Later in that same year another cross was given to Diana in the death of her brother Brancaleone. He had become *podestà* of Genoa; the annals of that city describe him as *miles formosus et sapiens,* a handsome and prudent soldier. Jordan wrote anxiously to her: "I feel that you are

[20] *Letter 10.*

16

very sad; but your sorrow shall be turned into joy, for according to the multitude of the sorrows in your heart the consolations of the Lord will give joy to you, and the Paraclete, whom the Father will send to you, will console you. I am sending brother Bernard to you, that he may be a comfort both to you and to the lady Jacobina;[21] and I beg and beseech him who consoles his own in all their sorrows that he may solace the heaviness of your hearts. For now, as we read in *Peter,* we must for a little time be made sorrowful that in somewhat we may be like to him who said, My soul is sorrowful even unto death. But after death we are to rejoice and make merry, for so we read that the just feast and rejoice before God, and sorrow and weeping are no more. And if you feel that your sorrow is perhaps a little excessive, then must you cry with the psalmist: Why art thou sad, O my soul, and why dost thou disquiet me? hope in God. Your brother has been snatched away; but it was lest wickedness should mar his understanding, or the deceits of this world should beguile his soul. Do not then let your sadness be excessive, my dearest ones, like those others who have no hope; your hope should be filled full of the immortality which is in you, and so you should beg the Lord to grant you joy of heart."[22]

Very soon afterwards he was writing to her again in the same sense: "You must know, beloved, that as the Scripture says, through many tribulations we must enter into the kingdom of God but when we have reached the kingdom we shall know sorrow no more; meanwhile your Bridegroom Jesus Christ will never desert you, for he hath said, I will not leave thee neither will I forsake thee; and this is true even though sometimes he may seem to be gone far from you so that you cry, Why, O Lord, hast thou retired afar off? why dost thou slight me *in opportunitatibus,* in times of want and weakness when help is needed and opportune? And when do we most need help if not, as the psalmist himself goes on to say, in the time of trouble? But certainly he will not then forsake you, he will draw nearer to you, for the Lord is nigh unto them that are troubled in heart.

"If then sometimes you are sad and go sorrowful whilst the enemy afflicteth you, think of the words of your Bridegroom who is the joy of angels, My soul is sorrowful even unto death; if pain afflict you, remem-

---

[21] Probably the wife of Brancaleone.
[22] *Letter 12.*

17

ber those other words, Attend and see if there be any pain like to my pain; for indeed he alone hath eyes for misery and sorrow. After labour there is rest for us; after suffering, everlasting consolation: according to the great multitude of our sorrows his comfort will rejoice our souls by his own gift who is your Bridegroom, who with his Father is blessed for ever. Amen.

"Do not abstain too much from food and drink and sleep; but in all things be moderate and patient."[23]

In March 1226, Jordan was back in Paris; and there he received news that caused him fresh anxiety for the little community of St. Agnes. Italy was in a state of turmoil; tension between Pope and Emperor was mounting; Bologna in particular had incurred the displeasure of Frederick II by its loyalty to the Holy See; the convent stood outside the walls of the city, and there were days of peril and dread when the imperial troops were passing near at hand.

"We have just heard," wrote Jordan, "of the troubles and distresses which afflict Bologna and therefore yourself and your sisters; and my grief is the greater inasmuch as I know I cannot in this matter give you any counsel or comfort except in so far as you can be helped by my prayers, sinner that I am, and by the prayers of our brethren, which I hope may be fruitful in the sight of God who is not wont to reject the prayers of his servants in their time of need nor be deaf to their supplications. Be not affrighted, therefore, beloved, nor lose heart, whatever trouble may befall, for you have a Bridegroom tried and tempered by all sorrows so that he knows how to compassionate with all sorrows, especially yours and those of his other brides.... Be nothing solicitous therefore, my daughter, but take courage and be valiant; for your Bridegroom is Emmanuel, God-with-us, who does not forsake those who trust in him but is with them as he promised even to the consummation of the world. Be tranquil then, casting all your care upon him whose power can never be vanquished, whose wisdom is never at fault, whose loving-kindness never wearies.... Think...upon him, who gave himself, not his brothers and sisters, to the onslaught of wickedness; and so you will not grow faint in soul."[24]

There was yet another cross which Diana and her sisters could not hope to escape: the dryness of soul that must come at times to all those

---

[23] *Letter 13.*   [24] *Letter 18.*

who try faithfully to seek God in the life of prayer. Diana, thinking of her unworthiness, was inclined to see in this a chastisement from God; Jordan is at pains to teach her otherwise. Less than a month later he wrote again from Paris, this time to all the sisters at St. Agnes,' "Be strengthened, beloved daughters, in the Lord Jesus your Bridegroom whom you have wisely chosen for yourselves above all the desirable things of the world, and whom, as I hope, you hold fast in the strong embrace of your prayers and tears lest he depart from you. Be not afraid therefore; for now no judgment stands against you since you have your Lord, the author of your salvation, who has the will and wisdom and power to free you from every distress and affliction and anguish of heart.

"Henceforth then, if any one of you be for a time cast down with weariness of spirit or afflicted with aridity of heart so that the torrent of devoted love seems to be dried up, will she dare to cry, My Lord hath forsaken me and hath no care for me, since the feelings of joy and devotion I have hitherto known are now gone from me?...Let them speak thus who know not his ways nor how, as I so often told you when I was with you, he is wont to kindle the love of his brides: how for a time he will draw away from you that you may seek him with greater ardour, and having sought may find him with greater joy, and having found may hold him with greater love, and having held may never let him go; like the bride in the *Song of Songs* who, after long searchings and questionings whether any had seen her beloved, at length when she had found him, exclaimed, I have held him and I will not let him go. And be comforted, you his brides, by the sweet words wherewith he answered one of his brides of whom Isaiah tells us, who was bewailing her dereliction...[and] the Lord replies to her: Can a woman forget her infant, so as not to have pity on the son of her womb? And if she should forget, yet will not I forget thee; for behold, I have graven thy image in the palms of my hands."[25]

Jordan returns to this same theme in a later letter to Diana written from Genoa in the summer of 1229, in which, after reassuring her about another trouble to which we shall come in a moment, he goes on: "For the rest, my beloved, be in all things confident and joyful; and what is lacking to you because I cannot be with you, make up for in the

---

[25] *Letter 20.*

company of a better friend, your Bridegroom Jesus Christ whom you have more constantly with you in spirit and in truth, and who speaks to you more sweetly and to better purpose, than Jordan. And if sometimes he seems to turn his face from you and become a stranger to you, you must see this not as a punishment but as a grace. He is the bond whereby we are bound together; in him my spirit is fast knit with your spirit; in him you are always without ceasing present to me wherever I may wander: he who is your Bridegroom Jesus Christ, God's Son, to whom is honour and empire everlasting, Amen."[26]

The earlier part of this same letter concerns a crisis which had long been impending and which perhaps caused Diana and her companions more anxiety than anything else. The trouble had begun in Germany; the friars there had, with more zeal than discretion, received into the Dominican nunneries crowds of applicants, many of them extremely unsuitable, and endless quarrels and dissensions had ensued. In consequence, many of the friars began to feel that they were being taken from the Order's main work of teaching and preaching because of the demands of the nuns for chaplains and advisers, and that it would be far better to put the monasteries under the care and jurisdiction of the bishops. But this meant in effect abandoning them and destroying the organic life of the Order as Dominic had envisaged it. Jordan, though deeply concerned for the teaching and preaching work of the friars, was against any such abandonment; but he put the matter before the General Chapter of the Order which met in Paris 1224, and also sought the opinion of the doctors of the University; and from both he received the same answer: they could not abandon the nuns when their care of them was a condition of the foundation of the monasteries, and a condition ratified by the Pope.[27]

For the moment then, all was well. But Diana feared that the subject would be re-opened; and in her fears for St. Agnes' she had recourse to the Pope and obtained from him a formal letter to the Master General, enjoining him to charge himself personally with the care of the convent. Her fears were justified. In 1228 there was held in Paris a *Capitulum Generalissimum* as it is called: a General Chapter of the Order with power

[26] *Letter 29.*

[27] [Pope Gregory IX (1145?-1241), a vigorous promoter of the mendicant orders and a devoted friend of St. Dominic. *Ed.*]

to make immediate permanent changes in the *Constitutions* of the Order. The whole matter was debated afresh; and the Chapter laid it down that the friars were not to be burdened with the direction of nunneries. This referred, not to the sisters of the Order, but to other monasteries. Unhappily, it was interpreted by some as meaning that the Chapter had spoken in favour of total abandonment of the sisters; and the provincial of Lombardy, Stephen, was one of those who held and propagated this view. In consequence, he caused Diana and her sisters a great deal of distress of mind; and Jordan, hearing of it, wrote him a letter which has a distinctly acid flavour. It appears that he had listened to the rumour-mongers who misinterpreted the Chapter's decree, and had swallowed unreflectingly what they told him; and thereupon he had been visited with scruples and had refused to admit to the habit of the Order those who were seeking admission to St. Agnes.'

"Your conscience has evidently been startled and affrighted at a mere rustle of leaves," wrote Jordan. "I know fully all the acts and decrees of all the Chapters, and the intentions of those who made the decrees; and I know that when this present law was passed the idea that it should refer to our own sisters was not only never raised, it was never thought of." He goes on to say that even had they wished to act thus they could not have done so, for they were bound by the orders of the Pope; there must be no further ambiguity therefore, the thing must not be called in doubt again; as for Stephen, he must "put aside all scrupulosity" and realize "the folly of changing one's views each time one hears a fresh opinion put forward."[28]

To Diana he wrote a letter of explanation and reassurance, the second half of which has already been quoted. "Don't worry," he says in effect; "be at peace"; *secure te habeas:* no harm can come to her from this new legislation.[29] But still the trouble was not finally over. During the General Chapter of 1235 Jordan was ill and could not be there; and legislation was passed ordering all those who were in charge of monasteries to go back to their priories. This time the oldest and most important monasteries, the ones founded by St. Dominic, Bologna included, appealed directly to Pope Gregory IX and their appeal was heard. There, as far as Diana's lifetime was concerned, the matter rested; later under Innocent IV the friars asked to be relieved of all their monaster-

[28] Appendix, *Letter 1.*   [29] Cf. *Letter 29.*

21

ies except Prouilhe and St. Sixtus, and again the nuns made representations to the Holy See, claiming rightly that without the care of the friars they would soon cease to be Dominicans in anything but the habit they wore, and the affair was finally settled in 1267 by Clement IV, who restored the original state of things and so saved the Order from what would have been a grave impoverishment of its life.

It was probably in or about the year 1229 that Diana's father died; and again Jordan wrote to console her. When death breaks friendships asunder, he told her, "those who are left to live on in this world weep and are sad for the death of their friends who go before them; but those who have died first do not mourn in the other world over the death of those who come after them. And you, beloved, you are long since dead with Christ if your life is hid with him in glory; therefore you have long since gone before your father into death and so you should not grieve for him, for if you do you must think of yourself as not yet fully dead with Christ. If I say this, it is not that your father's death...does not affect me: it does indeed, though principally on your account. But think with wonder of the gentleness of God...he takes from you what you could not hope to cling to for ever, only to give you what is eternal and shall never be taken away from you for ever.... Soon, if God wills, I shall see you all."[30]

If God wills...But it was the will of God that they should meet very seldom; and even so his visits were very brief. Jordan was a man of almost incredible energy and activity; his life as Master General was an incessant journey, mostly on foot, from end to end of Europe and beyond. So they were forced to say on paper what they would have wished to say face to face. The letters we have seen so far have been concerned with particular events, problems, distresses; but to read the whole series is to realize how constantly they were in each other's minds, so that the small events of every day, just as much as the major occurrences, are things about which they must tell each other.

"With Diana and her companions," writes Père Mortier, "but above all with Diana herself, his thoughts are incessantly occupied. Whether he is staying at Paris or at Padua, or trudging the roads of the world, the image of his beloved daughter follows him, haunts him, stirs him. If his efforts meet with success, if the students flock into the Order, if his

[30] *Letter 26.*

preaching wins to it famous Doctors, he writes to tell Diana. He tells her all: his joys and triumphs, his sorrows and disappointments; for he knows how keenly it will all interest her. Nor is it only of the things of the spirit that he tells her. This great man, so full of goodness of heart, descends to the minutest details of his life. He knows well enough how a woman's heart, however unworldly she may be, is made anxious by any suffering, physical or mental: it longs to know all that it may share all. If Jordan delays his letters Diana is sad or indeed impatient, and often he has to restore her serenity and peace of soul by tender reproaches. His long, perilous journeys, his delicate health make Diana always frightened for him: at the least onslaught of fever her whole soul is troubled. She knows the Master's austerity with himself; she knows that fatigue never stops him; and all the time she is frightened for his life. So these letters, these wonderful letters that one cannot read without deep emotion, follow one another at every halting place, to reassure her and console her."[31]

There was an occasion when Diana had hurt her foot, and told him of it; and he replied in a phrase which, as Père Mortier notes, was afterwards to cause such admiration in one of Madame de Sévigné's[32] letters. *Pedi tuo quern laesum intellexi, patior,* he wrote; and Mortier translates, *Je souffre à votre pied:* Your poor foot hurts me. But more often it was about his own health that he had to reassure her, and sometimes to scold her. "I am not happy about what I hear of you," he wrote to her in 1231, "that you are so troubled and anxious about my illness. Would you have me taken from the number of the sons of God and be in no wise a sharer in the passion of our Redeemer Christ Jesus? Do you not know that the Lord scourgeth every son whom he receiveth? And would you not have me received among his sons? Is your zealous concern for me then truly worthy? If you would have me enter the kingdom you must suffer me to travel the road that leads to the kingdom, for through many tribulations we must enter there. If this illness were to be to my hurt in any way then indeed I should be glad that you are dis-

---

[31] Mortier, Daniel Antonin (1858–?), *Histoire des maîtres généraux de l'Ordre des Frères Prêcheurs,* (Paris: A. Picara, 1903), vol. 1, p. 167.

[32] [Marie du Rabutin-Chantal, Marquise de Sévigné (1626–1696), seventeenth century woman of letters whose correspondence described life in the French salons and court. *Ed.*]

tressed by it; but if it is good and fruitful for me, how could I want you, beloved, to be distressed by that good?

"Wherefore, if you wish me to be consoled, if you wish to remove the cause of my anxiety concerning you, cast out sadness from your own heart and be more readily consolable; simply commend me to the Lord and beg him that whatever pain the future may hold for me it may be turned into a means of my correction. The good and gentle Craftsman knows how greatly the clay for his handiwork stands in need of refining: it is for us to submit ourselves in all things to his will, and leave all our ways in his hands…. Certainly here in the misery of our present sojourning the evils of sin come near to us; and since the sinner must again and again feel the lash it is not surprising if here we are scourged for our wickedness. I am ready then for scourges, if only I may thereby reach that resting-place which is God and to which no scourge can draw near, for no evil of sin can enter there, can enter those serene and shining dwellings into which may you and I together be gathered by the loving-kindness of him who is gentle and good, God's Son Jesus Christ who is blessed for ever and ever, Amen."[33]

An earlier letter, written from Trent in the summer of 1225, refers both to her anxiety over him and to his anxiety over her; it begins with a touchingly simple admission: "I do not requite your love fully; of that I am deeply convinced: you love me more than I love you. But I cannot bear you to be so afflicted in body and distressed in mind by reason of this love of yours which is so precious to me: and I have indeed heard that you are too oppressed and troubled because of my illness, you and your sisters too. In fact, however, your prayer has entered into the sight of the Lord and in his mercy he has accorded me a further span of life, or rather a time for repentance…. But I am anxious about you and your sisters; anxious to know what things are against you. Beloved daughter, be constant and trust in the Lord: no matter what trials vex you, what difficulties beset you on every side, God is in the midst of you all and therefore you must not be disquieted."[34]

The troubles that surrounded her were many and hard to bear; but above them and through them all there was the constant sorrow of her separation from him, the keener pain of their partings. In the spring of 1231 he wrote to her: "When I have to part from you I do so with

[33] *Letter 40.*   [34] *Letter 15.*

heavy heart; yet you add sorrow to my sorrow since I see you then so inconsolably weighed down that I cannot but be saddened not only by our separation which afflicts us both but also by your own desolation as well. Why are you thus anguished? Am I not yours, am I not with you: yours in labour, yours in rest; yours when I am with you, yours when I am far away; yours in prayer, yours in merit, yours too, as I hope, in the eternal reward? What would you do if I were to die? Certainly not even for my death should you weep so inconsolably. For were I to die you would not be losing me; you would be sending me before you to those shining dwellings [which God has established], that I abiding there might pray for you to the Father and so be of much greater use to you there, living with the Lord, than here in this world where I die all the day long."[35]

There are other letters in which he attempts to console her, not by minimizing his own sorrow but simply by pointing onwards to happier lands. "Let it not be a heavy burden on you, beloved," he had written already in 1229, "that I cannot all the time be with you in the flesh, for in spirit I am always with you in love unalloyed. Yet I cannot wonder that you are sad when I am far from you since, do what I may, I myself cannot but be sad that you are far from me; but I console myself with the thought that this separation will not last for ever: soon it will be over, soon we shall be able to see each other, endlessly, in the presence of God's Son Jesus Christ who is blessed for ever."[36]

Elsewhere he is concerned only to reassure her of his love and his constant awareness of her. "Beloved, I can write to you only very hurriedly; yet I had to try to write you something, however brief, in the hope of giving you if I can a little joy. You are so deeply engraven on my heart that the more I realize how truly you love me from the depths of your soul, the more incapable I am of forgetting you and the more constantly you are in my thoughts; for your love of me moves me profoundly, and makes my love for you burn more strongly. I must end this letter abruptly; but may he who is the supreme Consoler and Paraclete, the Spirit of Truth, possess and comfort your heart; and may he grant us to be with one another for ever in the heavenly Jerusalem, through the grace of our Lord Jesus Christ."[37]

[35] *Letter 35.* [36] *Letter 28.* [37] *Letter 25.*

Finally, there is a letter written some time in 1236—perhaps the last letter he ever wrote to her—in which there is no longer any distinction of intensity in his mind between his love and hers. Perhaps indeed his love for her had grown during these years until it equalled hers; and now—had he a presentiment of what was to come?—as he writes, his words become a simple undisguised outpouring of the longing of his heart. "Beloved, since I cannot see you with my bodily eyes nor be consoled with your presence as often as you would wish and I would wish, it is at least some refreshment to me, some appeasement of my heart's longing, when I can visit you by means of my letters and tell you how things are with me, just as I long to know how things are with you, for your progress and your gaiety of heart are a sweet nourishment to my soul—though you for your part do not know to what ends of the earth I may be journeying and even if you knew you would not have messengers to hand by whom you could send something to me. Yet whatever we may write to each other matters little, beloved: within our hearts is the ardour of love in the Lord whereby you speak to me and I to you continuously in those wordless outpourings of charity which no tongue can express nor letter contain.

"O Diana, how unhappy this present condition of things which we must suffer: that we cannot love each other without pain and anxiety! You weep and are in bitter grief because it is not given you to see me continually; and I equally grieve that it is so rarely given me to be with you. Who shall bring us into the strong city, into the city of the Lord of Hosts that the Highest himself hath founded, where we shall no more have to long either for him or for one another? Here on earth we are wounded every day and our hearts are torn to shreds; and every day our miseries cause us to cry out, Who shall deliver us from the body of this death?

"But no: these things we must bear with patience and, so far as our daily work allows, dwell in mind and heart with him who alone can deliver us from our distresses, in whom alone is rest, apart from whom we shall find nothing but misery and abundance of sorrow wheresoever we look. Meanwhile then let us accept with joy whatever sad things may come to us; for with what measure our trials are meted to us, so shall be measured our joy, poured out upon us by God's Son Jesus

Christ, to whom is honour and glory and strength and empire for ever and ever, Amen."[38]

"Who will bring us into the strong city, the city of the Lord of Hosts?" It was no new thing for either of them, this desire to see the God they loved above everything and to live that eternal life in which once and for all every sorrow is turned into joy; but for Diana, in the early days of her religious life, there had been one thing that held back her desire for the city of God: her work had not been completed, her convent of St. Agnes was not yet securely established. In this respect it is the year 1227 that marks a dividing line. We have seen something of the difference of opinion which divided the friars themselves on the subject of the direction of the monasteries of sisters; in December 1226 the matter was settled, primarily for St. Agnes' but also for all the other Dominican monasteries, by a bull addressed to Jordan by Pope Honorius III which placed these monasteries definitively under the direction of the Order. True, there were to be more difficulties later on, as we have seen, owing to the misunderstanding of the statute promulgated by the Chapter of 1228; but the principle was established, the authority of the Holy See was behind it; Jordan, on receiving the bull, forwarded it to Diana to be kept in the archives of St. Agnes'; she could feel that at last her work was completed.

With the bull Jordan sent a short covering letter of rejoicing. "I know well how, as we learn from the holy prophets of old and in these latter days from Paul through whom Christ hath spoken to us, we should rejoice with the servants of the Lord Jesus, and particularly in their own consolation and joy. Wherefore, having just had news of the consolation wherewith you and your sisters have been consoled by the favour you have now been granted,[39] I rejoice with you all, whose joy is my own.

"Beloved daughter, you know that hitherto I have always and in every place been with you, desiring and seeking your good and that of all your sisters; but now, for the future, I shall with God's grace be yet more solicitous for you. I commit to your care the letter which the Sovereign Pontiff entrusted to me for you: guard it well."[40]

---

[38] *Letter 50.*
[39] She knew already of the Pope's decision; the bull would seal and ratify her joy.
[40] *Letter 21.*

And later in the same year he wrote again: "You tell me…that you did not wish to die and enter into your Father's house where there are many mansions until the convent of St. Agnes had been fully established and confirmed under the jurisdiction of the Order but that now this is done you feel more carefree, and long to be dissolved and be with Christ. Certainly I want you to have this longing in your inmost heart; but I would not have you try to hasten its fulfilment by scrupulous searchings of conscience or immoderate bodily disciplines, for as Solomon tells us, he that is hasty, his feet shall stumble. Take care then not to run with so much haste that you grow faint in the way; as the apostle says, you must so run, in so well ordered a manner, that you may obtain the prize."[41]

The convent of St. Agnes then was securely established. What sort of life was lived there by Diana and her companions? They had been taught the primitive rule as it was observed at St. Sixtus' in Rome: what they were to strive after above all in their community life was a union of hearts, *cor unum et anima una,* to have one mind and one heart in the Lord; they were to hold all things in common; they were to be uniform in their observance of the common rules. One of the most important elements in their daily life was to be the carrying out of the Church's liturgy, the Divine Office, with greater or less solemnity according to the calendar; and that this might be the more fervent there was to be time set aside every day for private prayer, in the hour after Compline[42] and again after Matins,[43] though in this latter case they were to see to it that the sisters' rest should not be disturbed by any of them coming late to the *dormitorium.*[44] They were to be tireless at work, for idleness is the enemy of the soul; at table their minds were to be occupied with reading; their life was to be one of poverty, and the rule enjoined that a sister who grumbled about food or clothing was to be deprived for forty days of the thing grumbled about.

From these and similar rules a clear picture emerges of the life at St. Agnes' as a realization of the original ideal of St. Dominic. That ideal is

---

[41] *Letter 22.*

[42] [Night Prayer. Last of the seven canonical hours prayed before retiring. *Ed.*]

[43] [Liturgical office and the first of the seven canonical hours; traditionally prayed at midnight or sunrise. *Ed.*]

[44] [Sleeping quarters where the cells (rooms) of the nuns were located. *Ed.*]

sketched in its salient features by Père Cormier: the convent was to be like a city of the poor, with numerous dwellings, varied therefore but with its variety welded into a unity by the order which prevails within it; a city of the poor but whose poverty does not exclude a certain beauty; a city whose life is made up of the twofold movement of Jacob's ladder—the divine life coming down into the midst of the inhabitants and transfiguring all their activities; their own religious life mounting to God in worship and praise. To help them the more easily to turn all their activities into worship and love there is the daily liturgy, the Divine Office; there are the religious practices of penance and of obedience, the hidden life in the cells, the rule of silence; above all there is the soul of their community life, the pure, sincere, effortless superabundance of their charity.

Thus there is realized in the cloister, unhindered, unrestrained, joyfully, gaily—*on dirait presque en se jouant*—the union of natural goodness and supernatural grace. And over all there is the indefinable, unanalyzable family spirit: that union of hearts which makes all things one without effacing any of the individual characteristics and qualities of the members of the family but on the contrary freeing all that is good in those characteristics from the stifling teguments of selfishness and causing them to shine all the more brightly.[45]

That ideal of achieving a fusion between family unity and the fulfillment of individual gifts and qualities is of the essence of Dominican life. The religious community, like the Church, is as a human body, composed of many members each with its own function and therefore the qualities necessary to fulfill that function: the family life is made up of the use of the gifts which each one brings to it; and in return those gifts themselves are perfected through their use for the good of the family. Diana herself had her own very distinctive gifts; and as her religious life went on she learned with Jordan's help and guidance how to free them from what was imperfect in them, how to use them for her religious family's progress in goodness and peace and happiness, how to make them a more and more perfect offering to God from whom they came. She remained to the end Diana: it is Père Cormier again who notes how

[45] Cf. H.-M. Cormier, O.P., *La bienheureuse Diane d'Andalò et les bienheureuses Cécile et Amate, fondatrices du couvent de Sainte-Agnès de l'Ordre des Frères-Prêcheurs à Bologne* (Rome: Imprimerie de la Propagande, 1892), pp. 74-76.

she and the two other members of the community who were beatified with her personify the three essential graces of monastic life: Amata, deep humility; Cecilia, the prioress, wise and creative authority; Diana, the greatest grace of them all, perfect love.

It was that power of love, strengthened, deepened, hallowed by the divine life within her, that Jordan was most concerned to guard and to guide.

He had to warn her, first, against the excessive penances to which her zeal and her sense of sin prompted her: if zeal is to be perfect it must be an expression of wisdom: the wisdom that understands the end and can establish in their right measure the means that lead to it. Then he must fill her mind and heart more and more with the thought of that end: help her to live more and more closely in the company of Christ her Bridegroom, to find more and more joy in the thought of the heavenly Jerusalem which awaited her. "My eyes are ever towards the Lord": this constantly recurring theme finds with equal frequency its two complementary applications in the doctrine of wise moderation in the practice of bodily penance, and in the ideas of joy, gaiety, peace and the refusal to be disturbed by every fleeting adversity or even by sorrows and troubles that are grave.

One of Jordan's earliest letters to her, written from Paris in the winter of 1223, gives us a magnificent summary of this teaching. His journey had been interrupted by a lengthy illness, but now he has arrived and is in good health, and he hastens to write to her that she may "at least have the solace of a greeting by letter" since for the time being he cannot be with her and talk with her. "Apply yourselves with all your might," he tells her and her sisters, "not so much to bodily penances, in which the measure of wisdom and prudence can easily be exceeded, as to the life of virtue and the practice of that godliness which according to the apostle is profitable to all things. Let your hearts be always filled with a burning desire for the blessed city of the saints in paradise, that glorious storeroom of perfect joy and gladness, that abode of light, radiant with the splendour of utter beauty, far exceeding the understanding of man: a realm truly divine, worthy to be the dwelling place of him who is created in the image and likeness of God. Let the loving thought of the Bridegroom be constantly in your minds; and, as his eyes are upon you, do all you can to make your beauty perfect before him, ridding yourselves of any stain or blemish however small that might sully it and offend his divine gaze. Let there be purity in your hearts and innocence in your lives; in all that you do, be of one mind and one heart, in peace and concord, in unshakeable love, and in that loving humility which is the guardian of all good things; so that, while your souls find deep and lasting delight in the life of holiness, they may themselves be a source of delight to the Son of God who is blessed for ever and ever."[46]

In the early summer of 1225, on his way from Bologna to Germany, he writes again to all the sisters of St. Agnes,' and his theme is joy, his prose more completely and intricately than usual a tapestry woven of threads from Scripture and liturgy. "My daughters are decked out and adorned indeed, but not like those daughters of men of whom the psalmist speaks who are adorned round about after the similitude of a temple and in whom in truth there is the similitude but not the sanctitude. The temple of God is holy, and you are that temple; nor is there any doubt but that the Lord is in his holy temple, dwelling within you…. Yet a little while and my daughters shall be brought to the King our Lord, shall be brought to him with gladness and rejoicing. They shall be brought after her who is the queen, after Mary, the chosen one, his Maiden-Mother…into the temple of the King;…and there, as Isaiah said, the bridegroom shall rejoice over the bride and your God shall rejoice over you.

"You shall come into Sion with praise, and everlasting joy shall be upon your heads—that everlasting crown which is called joy because it is the fullness of all bliss. You shall receive a kingdom of glory and a crown of beauty at the hand of the Lord; for it is then that he will say to his faithful servant, Enter thou into the joy of thy Lord…and so all your sorrow shall be turned into joy, and your joy no man shall take from you."[47]

In the following year he urges them all once again to use a wise discretion in journeying to the city of God and its eternal joys. "Beloved daughters, though you run after your Bridegroom, drawn by the fragrance of his ointments, see to it that you tread circumspectly, that you so run that you may obtain the prize, being neither laggard and slow to run, nor so hasty that your feet stumble and you fail to reach your goal.

[46] *Letter 8.*   [47] *Letter 11.*

31

Narrow and strait indeed is the way that leadeth to life; so you must go forward warily lest you stray from it to the one side through lack of diligence and fervour or to the other side through excessive austerity. In your case it is the second of the two dangers that I fear the more: I fear lest, unwisely chastising your flesh, you should fall into worse calamity and find yourselves hindered in the way of the Lord, the way leading to that city which is your home, the city of the Lord of Hosts which God hath founded for ever...The way to this city is indeed hazardous; but when it shall be given to us to reach [it]...then there will be no more dangers to fear: nothing there to bring about ruin, but only eternal peace, eternal stability, eternal security....

"Meanwhile, for as long as we must toil along the road let us go forward not with unwise impetuosity but with prudence....

"Beloved daughters, if any trouble or sorrow come upon you, bear all with patience and evenness of temper, awaiting the time when for small troubles endured you shall be given great glory, for sorrow joy, for mourning everlasting comfort."[48]

It was natural that Jordan should be constantly concerned to turn Diana's thoughts to the joy of heaven: the life at St. Agnes' was a hard one, quite apart from her own personal crosses. But we should wholly misread his teaching if we thought of it in terms of a black and white contrast between this world and the next: here a gloomy quest for pain and sorrow with the idea of obtaining there a brilliant reward. Such an idea was as alien to his spirit as it had been to St. Dominic's and as it is today to the spirit of his Order. We misunderstand the Christian ideal if we confuse hardness with unhappiness. Christianity bids us do things that are hard; it is no enemy to happiness. Some of the greatest natural joys of life are to be found in activities that are hard, that imply a good deal of going against the grain: the discipline of art, the austerities of athlete or explorer, the self-sacrifice of a life dedicated to science, the devoted self-giving of all true friends and lovers. Our Lord was at pains to make this clear to us: Happy are the poor in spirit, he said: he was stating a fact.

Miserliness and avarice, clinging to what we have, grasping after what we covet, trying to pretend that we and not God are the lords of creation: this is, for fallen human nature, the easy way, but it is the way

[48] *Letter 19.*

to unhappiness, to endless worry and anxiety, to fear and frustration, to pain, rage, loneliness. Poverty of spirit is the hard way: it is hard to admit not only in theory but in practice that all things are God's, not ours, and that it is for him and not for us to dispose of them; but if we succeed it is freedom that we find, and with freedom, fullness of life, and fullness of life is happiness. If we are poor, humble and obedient we can accept our creatureliness fully in our hearts and act accordingly, can accept the will of God in everything because it is God that we love in everything—and this is the highest form of freedom, the freedom demanded by love that it may be able to serve what it loves. So St. Paul tells us that the fruits of the spirit are love, joy, peace: the love that makes our wills one with the will of God whom we love, then the joy and peace that must follow from the fact that self will and its tensions, anxieties, fears, revolts have been swallowed up in love.

This joy, the joy that even here and now in this world is found underlying all the sorrows of life in the souls of the lovers of God, is at the heart of Jordan's teaching. Indeed we can see it appearing first of all in the very materials—the natural human materials—out of which the Dominican life is to be built. The life of the convent, as we have seen, has to be a life of poverty, but a poverty not excluding a certain beauty; the virtues of religious life have to be coloured through and through by the family spirit which keeps them fresh and homely and humanly attractive. Jordan himself was not only famous for his own personal joy-ousness: he was always preaching joy, and had been known to rebuke a thin-lipped friar for scolding some novices who had laughed during Divine Office—and had they not good cause to be happy, Jordan demanded. He himself had experience enough of toil and sorrow; but he had wisdom and love enough to enable the sorrow to be turned into joy. Poverty, humility, love, are words which for him mean, even on earth, richness and joy and fullness of life.

In 1223 he was still worried about the future of St. Agnes,' for Honorius III was refusing to allow him to take sisters from St. Sixtus' to help with the new foundation; moreover he had been ill; yet he found time to write Diana a letter about these three virtues which is a song of triumph.

"You have contemned the kingdom of this world and all its pomps for the love of Jesus Christ your beloved Bridegroom; you have chosen and taken to yourself his poverty; so you shall dwell in his courts and be filled with the good things of his house. But what am I saying? Is it really poverty that you have chosen? Rather it is poverty that you have thrown aside and riches that you have chosen; for the poverty of Christ is a willed poverty, that poverty of spirit which gives you the kingdom of heaven. I do not say which *will* give you the kingdom: it gives it you here and now; your Bridegroom himself tells us, Happy are the poor in spirit, for theirs *is* the kingdom of heaven. To have the poverty of Christ is to count all the treasures of the world as nothing: is not this then the greatest of all treasures since in comparison with it and because of it all other riches are regarded as worthless and counted as poverty? You are not needy, for you abound in the glory and wealth of his house; you, who have the kingdom of heaven, are not a poor little woman but a queen, the queen of a realm.

"Stand then at the right hand of your Bridegroom, in vesture of gold, in vesture of love unfeigned, white and ruddy in its ardour and fervour for Christ. And where shall you find the gold wherewith to gild your clothing? Where but in the land of Hevilath, which means the land of sorrow? In that land is Christ, who calls to us: Attend and see if there be any sorrow like to my sorrow. There you shall find gold; and the gold you shall find in that land is very precious since it is there that Christ shows us the perfection of love: for greater love no man hath than this, that he lay down his life for his friends.... Let this then be the object of all your thought, your care, your toil; for it is here that you will find the gold of the Arabians, that is, of the humble...because it is only the humble who can search it out and find it and gather it, for they alone can enter these deep and narrow mines. Be humble and small then in your own eyes, for it is to the little ones that God gives understanding, to the humble that he gives his grace. May he then give you understanding, and instruct you in the way which you should go, and fix his eyes upon you, for his eyes look upon the poor.

"Thus briefly have I commended to you poverty, love, and humbleness of heart, that by means of these you may come to true riches and joys and honours, through the help of him who is a strong helper, our Lord Jesus Christ who is blessed for ever and ever."[49]

---

[49] *Letter 7.*

Then there is a Christmas greeting, sent at a time when Jordan was overwhelmed with work, in which with even more than his usual charm of thought and diction he expresses the same theme of joy in Christ. "I cannot find the time to write you the long letter your love would wish for and I would so gladly send; none the less I do write, I send you a very little word, the Word made little in the crib,[50] the Word who was made flesh for us, the Word of salvation and grace, of sweetness and glory, the Word that is good and gentle, Jesus Christ and him crucified, raised up on the Cross, raised in praise to the Father's right hand: to whom and in whom do you raise up your soul and find there your rest unending for ever and ever. Read over this Word in your heart, turn it over in your mind, let it be sweet as honey on your lips; ponder it, dwell on it, that it may dwell with you and in you for ever.

"There is another word that I send you, small and brief: my love, which will speak for me to your love in your heart and will content it. May this word too be yours, and likewise dwell with you for ever."[51]

The first fruit of the love poured into our hearts by the Spirit is joy; the second is peace. There are precious lines in which Jordan deals with peace as Christianity understands it, that peace which the world cannot give but which love can give. In 1229 he had been making one of his prolonged journeys through France, Switzerland, Germany; he had found the peace of his Order disturbed by calumnies and enmities; at the same time the tranquility of St. Agnes' was menaced by the war in Italy. He wrote to the community: "I exhort you, beloved daughters, that with earnest prayer you beseech God the author of peace to grant unity in his peace to the holy Church; for throughout the world wars and seditions rage, putting many souls in peril of eternal damnation; and do you, dear daughters, knowing this, burn the more ardently with love of your Bridegroom who has snatched you from the turmoil of the world and established you in his peace; established you so firmly that even though trouble or distress come upon you from without, the peace within you should rather be increased than lessened, so long as you are patient in all things.

"And indeed there is nothing that can come upon you whether of good or of adverse fortune that you should not learn to accept with

---

[50] The *breve verbum de verbo abbreviato* of St. Bernard of Clairvaux; cf. *infra*, p. 95.
[51] *Letter 31.*

tranquil mind, fixing your hearts on the Lord by whose unfailing help we can make light of prosperity and be fearless in face of adversity. I hope that you abound in all good things in the Lord; and may he from whose hands these gifts come to you be pleased to preserve them and cause them ever to increase in richness within you."[52]

Some five years later, in the letter which mentions the dream he had had about her, he writes to Diana of the peace of Christ as indeed the beginning of beatitude, the beginning of that life in which distress over the past and anxiety for the future are alike swept away and there remain only the joy and tranquility of the eternal present. "Beloved, you know well in your wisdom how for as long as we are detained in the exile of this world we are all burdened by innumerable defects and cannot arrive at that stability which will be given us in the world to come, so that we fail to accept with equal mind all that befalls us, being sometimes too elated by good fortune, sometimes too much cast down by bad. It should not be so: since our desire is to attain to immortal life in the future we ought even now to conform ourselves in some measure to that future life, establishing our hearts in the strength of God and striving with all our might to fix on him all hope, all trust, all stability of purpose, so as to become like to him, who remains always firm and unmoved in himself. He is that secure refuge, never failing, always abiding, whereto the more we flee, the more steadfast we become in ourselves; whence it is that the saints, who had so great a trust in the Lord, were able so easily to make light of whatever misfortunes befell them.

"Do you therefore, beloved, more and more flee to him; then, no matter what hardship or sorrow may befall you, your heart will be established upon so solid and firm a foundation that it will never be moved. Think often of this and impress it deeply upon your heart; and urge your sisters to do likewise."[53]

In these later years of Jordan's life the Order was growing and spreading rapidly; his labours were becoming more and more onerous, his journeys more prolonged. Hence his visits to Bologna had to be more and more rare. It is not surprising therefore to find in the letters he wrote her towards the end an insistence on complete self-dedication to, and union with, God, whose "will is our peace." But in a deeper sense too it is fitting that the later letters should stress this theme, since

[52] *Letter 30.*   [53] *Letter 46.*

it is the crowning idea of all Jordan's teaching. "My eyes are ever towards the Lord": the rules, the discipline, the austerities, of religious life are to be seen as means to an increase of virtue; but all virtue, in the Christian sense, is meant to be an expression of love; and what is the essence of love but the identification of the lover's will with that of the beloved?

Jordan therefore is constantly concerned to preserve his daughters from the danger of making asceticism an end in itself (which is to fix the eyes not on God but on the self), or of turning it through imprudence and excess not into a means to greater virtue and greater love but into a hindrance, weakening the body and so robbing the personality of the energy and zest it needs for its journey to God. With the virtues on the other hand, he is always telling them, there is no need to fear excess:[54] they cannot be too humble, too great-hearted, too pure; but here too they must make sure that their eyes are always on the Lord, their virtues an expression not of concern for themselves but of love for him; and that love must be for them, even in this world, a beginning of the life of eternity with its unshakeable joy and peace, because it must mean always more and more fully, deeply, unreservedly, a living in Christ and his will, a sharing of his heart, a total and glad acceptance of his way in everything because it *is* the will of love.

In the early months of 1235 he was at Paris. It was a long time since he and Diana had seen each other. "The longer we are separated from one another," he wrote to her, "the greater becomes our desire to see one another again. Yet it is only by God's will (as I hope) that so far I have been prevented from coming to you; and if this was his will, it is for us to bend ours to conformity with it."[55] He went on to say that now, however, he would soon be seeing her; meanwhile he briefly reassured her about his health, though he added that he was suffering a good deal with one of his eyes and was in danger of losing it.

But in fact he was not to reach Bologna as he had hoped; and so he wrote again, this time to all the sisters: "As you see, by God's will I have again been prevented from attending the General Chapter; and even had I no other cause for distress I should be sad simply because of you, because you above all I cannot see, nor find comfort in being with you. But we must bear with patience what our God ordains for us. In every

---

[54] Cf. *infra, Letter 24.* [55] *Letter 48.*

possible way he makes plain to you how in this life we are not to fix our hopes on man nor seek our consolation in mortal things: he it is whom we are to love with our whole heart and our whole soul and our whole strength, since only in him can we and ought we to find our sufficiency, in this life by his grace and in the life to come by his glory. In all things then, dear daughters, be constant and joyful and prudent, that you be counted not among the foolish virgins but among the wise. I have not the time to write more to you now; but I commend you all, body and soul, to his mercy in whose hands are all the ends of the earth, who is blessed for ever."[56]

"In whose hands are all the ends of the earth"...Jordan was soon to journey to those ends of the earth, perhaps without seeing her again. But she for her part had fulfilled her destiny. She had done her work as a foundress, true to the ideals of Dominic: her convent was established, an organic part of the life of the Order. She had done her work as a Dominican of the Second Order: her prayers had sustained Jordan and his friars in their trials, made intercession for them in their ventures, praised and thanked God for them in their successes. She had done her work, finally, as the Diana of the letters: her love had given Jordan strength, comfort, joy through his many cares and troubles. It had done more: it had called forth from his own heart a flowering, a fullness of life, which helped to make his greatness, helped to make him what he was, what the Order needed, and God wanted, him to be. Now not only he but she too would soon be going, though by different ways, to the ends of the earth and beyond; but still even there, as all through their long separations, they would be hand in hand because by God's grace they had seen to it that their hands, like those same ends of the earth, were in this life and for ever in his.[57]

Nature abhors a vacuum: terrible things can happen to a man with an empty heart. That is one reason why it can be more difficult for a priest or a religious to be a good Christian, living a really vital Christian life, than for happily married lay people. These can without too much

---

[56] *Letter 49.*

[57] The remaining paragraphs of this section are adapted from an article, "Love Among the Saints," published in *Life of the Spirit*, August-September 1953, by kind permission of the editor.

difficulty integrate their love of each other into their shared love of God, sanctifying the one and deepening the other. What of the priest and the religious?

One sometimes meets among lay people a dangerously romanticized idea of this vocation. For them, these are men and women set apart, dedicated, living in the sanctuary, their whole lives spent close to God, their minds and hearts filled with God, and with a charity which causes them to think of all other human beings merely as "souls" to be served and saved. And to move the more sentimental there is that painting of the young monk with cowled head gazing wistfully through the narrow gothic window of his tiny cell at the world he has lost for ever....

What are the facts? A youth leaves school or university and enters a novitiate. Like every other youth he has family, relatives, friends, various interests; he is the normal untidy mixture of good and bad qualities; and as he crosses the threshold of the monastery no sudden transformation will take place within him: he remains what he was before: all that he changes is his clothes.[58] Now he enters upon a long course of training and studies: intellectually arduous and, unless there is extraordinarily wise guidance, psychologically dangerous in the extreme. Dangerous to the whole of the emotional side of his nature: inevitably he is more or less cut off from his previous normal human contacts with family and friends, with the familiar matter-of-fact daily life of the world, with the normal avocational necessities, sport, films, novels, parties, dances. Then, unless he has joined a purely contemplative order, he returns, when his studies are completed, to life in the world: he will probably be given a job which he will find humanly speaking interesting, perhaps absorbing, though like most human jobs it is hard work; and all the time he will once again be meeting people.

The importance of these two last points is this: that it is unlikely that his human interests and attitudes of mind will have been wholly replaced by the divine; and that one does not need to have lived a lifetime behind a wall to find oneself more or less maladjusted emotionally to a renewal of human contacts and personal relationships. It is here

[58] Obviously the divine power and vitality we call grace can and does make up for defects both of temperament and of training; but we cannot normally expect miracles, and have to take into account the natural human material from and in which grace must work.

39

that two opposite dangers can confront the young priest: of becoming either too immersed in, or too remote from and out of sympathy with, human affairs; and it is not surprising if he becomes involved in the one or the other—indeed, if we are to be realists we must admit that practically every priest and religious will fail to some extent in one direction or the other, for the only people who do not fail at all in this are the saints.

A great—indeed a frightening—responsibility for what will in fact follow rests of course on those directing the previous years' training: great because there is no exaggerating the good that can be achieved by a really wise guidance; frightening because there is no exaggerating the havoc that folly may cause. Just as a foolish direction can ruin a young man's health, both physically and psychologically, in the sacred name (in this case the *sacré nom*) of asceticism or religious fervour; just as a false theory of obedience can give him a wholly wrong outlook on life by training him to identify the ideal with the unnatural; just as he may have his youthful gaiety extinguished in him for the sake of a stuffy decorum, or his individuality quenched by the imposition of a common pattern, a sort of universal pseudo-personality; so too his emotional nature, his heart, may be wholly repressed and smothered, the lid firmly screwed down, while all his energies are directed to the avoidance of any wrongdoing, so that he ends in a sort of irreproachable vacuum. (Sometimes this last is justified on the grounds of playing for safety: but safety for what? and at what price? In the last resort it is better to run the risk of an occasional scandal than to have a monastery—a choir, a refectory, a recreation room—full of dead men. Our Lord did not say "I am come that ye may have safety, and have it more abundantly." Some of us would indeed give anything to feel safe, about our life in this world as in the next, but we cannot have it both ways: safety or life, we must choose).

This sort of training may, if it is sufficiently powerful, determine a personality in this way once and for all. One does meet priests and religious who are obviously good, and indeed holy, but who are in a curious way remote, aloof, "detached"; they will gladly expend their last energies on their official duties, they will do anything to help "souls," they will surely have a very bright crown in heaven; if you wanted an expert answer to some technical question about prayer or piety you would go to them unhesitatingly—but if you were struggling desperately with some purely human, personal problem you would never dream of approaching them. It means surely that though they are holy they are not saints; they are not, humanly speaking, examples of perfect holiness; and they are not saints precisely because there is something *human* lacking to them, their hearts are not fully alive, they have not yet fully realized in themselves the ideal given us under the symbol of the sacred heart of Christ, his *human* love of men. You cannot think of our Lord not taking a vivid personal interest in his publicans and sinners, his friends, the children who flocked to him, any more than you can think of St. Vincent de Paul not taking a personal interest in his orphans and waifs, or St. Catherine of Siena in her wayward protégés, or St. Francis in all his protégés from Brother Leo to the sparrows. And of Jordan of Saxony it is enough to remember that as we have seen he was always known as *dulcis*, sweet-natured: he was no aloof, impersonal administrator.[59]

A type of training which kills the heart kills the possibility, humanly speaking, of perfect holiness. But it may only smother the heart temporarily; and then perhaps the opposite danger will threaten the priest as he takes his place again in the world. (Indeed, even if his training has been perfectly sound and wise he can hardly be expected to be already a saint when he is ordained, so that in this case also he will have to meet something of the same danger.) It is the danger of gradually allowing human interests to crowd out his love of God. He may become too wholly absorbed in the humanly interesting aspects—perhaps even the financial aspects—of his work; he may be led by reaction from his previous training, or quite simply by loneliness, into plunging too wildly into personal relationships; he may gradually lose his earlier fervour and begin to look about him for distractions of one sort or another.

Officially, the priesthood is a state set apart and dedicated; but priests are *people:* are human beings with the normal human tale of frailties and follies. If they keep their hearts alive and young in them they may fall into fresh follies; if they kill their hearts they will never reach

[59] Some people are temperamentally "aloof" in the sense of being shy of human contacts—and they may well achieve holiness precisely through the discipline of achieving that human approachability which their vocation demands of them. It is not with them that we are concerned here; but with those who regard—and, still worse, teach others to regard—an impersonal aloofness as the Christian ideal.

the full glory of their vocation and may well fall into worse disasters, into a living death. That is why the example of men like Jordan of Saxony can be so great a help.

The one essential thing for him is the love of God; as we have seen, there is never any uncertainty in these letters as to who must come first in Diana's heart. It is not Jordan himself, it is that "better friend" who speaks to her more sweetly and to better purpose than Jordan. The love of God comes first for both of them, though it brings them the sorrow of separation and of constant anxiety for each other. But at the same time it is precisely their shared love of God which binds them so closely together: "He is the bond whereby we are bound together: in him my spirit is fast knit with your spirit, in him you are always without ceasing present to me wherever I may wander."

We have seen, in the extracts from his letters already given, enough to convince us of the *humanness* of Jordan's holiness and of the human reality of his love for Diana: whether he is consoling her in her troubles or telling her of his, whether he is counselling or warning or pleading or simply telling her of the little details of his travels, always there is the same underlying depth of feeling for her which the constantly recurring *carissima, carissima mea,* only serve to emphasize. He cannot wonder that their separation fills her with sadness since it fills him with sadness too; when he has to part from her it is with heavy heart, but doubly so because of her own sorrow; the more he realizes how truly and wholly she loves him, the more incapable he is of forgetting her, the more often she is in his thoughts, for her love of him deepens and strengthens his love of her: the letters reveal clearly all the help that Jordan was giving Diana, but equally they reveal the help that she was giving him. That is why they are in effect such a wonderful treatise on Christian friendship. The principles emerge very clearly.

First, the human love is to be wholly integrated into the love of God and therefore made wholly obedient to the will of God. Secondly, if that is done it becomes a thing of joy, though also of sorrow, and a thing very precious in itself. But thirdly, it is more than that: it is also an immense *help:* a strengthening in times of difficulty, a consolation in times of distress, but also something more still: a positive help to the deepening and purifying of the personality in general and of the love of God in particular. The love of Jordan led Diana on and on towards the "strong city" where love is perfect in God; but also the love of Diana led Jordan on, called forth from his own heart a flowering, an extra fullness of life, which helped to make his greatness, helped to make him what he was and what the Order needed him to be. "Be constant, joyful and prudent" he tells Diana and her companions in one of the letters: it is not every spiritual teacher or director who would remember—or even think—to instruct his followers to be joyful. Jordan who, more than any one man after St. Dominic himself, created the *spirit* of the Order, gave to it a gaiety and an informality in its daily life which are amongst its greatest treasures, for they enshrine and express a whole theology of religious life....

Even so this is not quite all: it leaves something essential to be said. A love such as this does not merely give a man more to give to men: it gives him more to give to God.

This is not always clearly seen. Sometimes an intense and deep human love comes into a life which has hitherto been wholly wrapt up in the love of God. Then the question may be asked: Does this mean either that in the opening of my heart to this love I am being unfaithful to God, or that in sending it he is in some sense rejecting me? To which the answer is in both cases, no: the difficulty arises from the fact that you put the love of God and the love of man on a level, as though they were the same *kind* of love; but they are not. If a woman, happily married to a man she loves, finds her life invaded by a new love, perhaps of an intensity she had hitherto not dreamt of, she may well feel this sense of tension, of unfaithfulness, because the two loves, however different in intensity, are still essentially the same kind of love: not only the will but the emotions and senses are essentially engaged. But the love of God is essentially only in the will, though the other levels of the personality may incidentally be involved at times. That is why the test of whether you love God is not whether you feel very loving but whether you do his will.

Self-deception is all too easy: you could feel that you were given wholly to God, wrapt up in his love and his service, because you spent long hours in church and at prayer or in absorbing the works of the mystics, and all this might in fact be a form of self-indulgence: the test would be, Do I always do what *I* want to do, brushing aside all claims which conflict with my desires, or do I really love God and my fellow men not just emotionally but in deed and in truth? If then your emotions are elsewhere engaged, why should you take this to be inevitably a betrayal or a diminishing of your love of God? If your senses rejoice in colour or harmony or the sun's warmth on your body, do you love God the less? If great painting makes you catch your breath, if great music brings you near to ecstasy, if great poetry makes you cry, do you love God any the less? But, you retort, all these are quite different: the love of a human being is much more *dangerous*. So we return to the cult of safety.

More dangerous, yes: it is easy for some temperaments to become so absorbed in music or literature as to neglect their duties, it is much easier for most temperaments to become so absorbed in a human being as to neglect their duties. But danger is not the same as disaster: danger is a matter of degree, and a purely individual matter varying with each human being. If you love both a human being and music, are you to say you must reject the human love because that is more dangerous but you may keep the love of music because though dangerous it is less so? Or are you to outlaw everything? If so, what of the parable of the man who hid his talent in a napkin? What of the homely proverb, which applies to God as well as to men: Love me, love my dog? What of the idea of vocation, which means using for God the gifts that God has given you? You must be "constant, joyful, prudent": and of course where danger is greater, there prudence must be greater too. (But danger, let us be clear, essentially not of falling into this or that particular sin so much as of being absorbed, being led to turn away from God or to reject him, to cease to have your eyes ever on the Lord.)

At the bar of heaven shall we be expected only to say how we have done with our fasting and almsdeeds, our pursuit of virtue? Shall we not also be expected to say, You gave me a love of music, and I have tried a little to deepen and sanctify it: to love the magic you put into the souls of your children—John Sebastian and Wolfgang and Ludwig and Johannes—and to praise you through it; you gave me a love of words, and of the magic you make through men's lips, and I have tried not to belittle your gift; you gave me a love of colour, and I have tried to use your gift creatively in a sad, drab world? And shall we not, still more, be expected to say: You gave me, though unworthy, the love of these your children, to keep me young and joyful in heart and to help me in the dark places, and I tried to be prudent and to let no harm come thereby to them or to me, but also I tried not to disparage the gift nor refuse its responsibilities? Be constant, joyful, prudent: if like Jordan you have care for the widows and orphans and keep yourself unspotted from this world—if, in other words, you grow more and more free from egoism and greed and rapacity, then you have less and less cause for fear: you can find a better motive in all that you do than the cult of safety.

Be prudent. There is one very important question which helps to a prudential judgment: Does this love, whatever it is, make me less faithful and devoted to my *vocation?* does it take my mind and heart away from my work, my family, my prayers, the good I can do and ought to do in the world? If so, there is indeed something wrong. But it need not be so: and if you find on the contrary that through it your work is enriched, your prayer deepened, your family life made more joyful and tender, your work for men more wise and sympathetic and gentle, then you have nothing to do but to thank God: there is nothing more to be said.

Or rather, there is one thing more; and it appears very clearly in these letters. When God brings a human love to a soul who before loved only himself it is not a rejection of her love but the exact contrary: he is giving her more to love him with. He may well be asking something harder, more complicated, of her: he is certainly not asking something smaller. Every love you have—of nature, of art, of men, of wisdom—is an added way of loving and worshipping him, an additional gift to offer him. But that means in the last resort a gift to give back to him. For every love is a new joy but implies also a new sorrow, until that "strong city" is reached on which the hearts of Jordan and Diana were set. "Naked I came, said he, when I left my mother's womb, and whence I came, naked I must go." What prudence demands of us, and seldom has the lesson been more beautifully taught than in these letters, is that we should make our own those other words of Job, to be constantly with us: "The Lord gave, the Lord has taken away: blessed be the name of the Lord."

PART II

Letters to Diana

Advent 1222 to Easter 1224

A S Master General of his Order Jordan had to be constantly on the move, visiting the priories already established and founding new ones both in Europe and, latterly, "beyond the seas" as well. He also had to preside at the annual General Chapter; and we shall see the general pattern of his wanderings more clearly—and at the same time realize more clearly the vastness of them and the strain they must have put on him since apart from his sea voyages he travelled everywhere on foot—if we remember that these Chapters were held alternately at Paris and at Bologna: these were the two poles between which his visits to other priories and other countries had to be fitted in. It is not always possible to say exactly when and where he wrote his letters to Diana;[1] but with their help and that of other documents we can more or less follow the course of Jordan's journeys through the years from 1222 onwards.

The Chapter of 1222, at which Jordan was elected Master General, was held at Paris, in May; when that was over he presumably set out on a tour of the then existing houses of the Order, planning his journey so as to be in Bologna in time for the next Chapter, at Bologna, the following Whitsuntide.[2] His letters are often coloured by allusions to the current liturgy of feast or season: the reference in *Letter 1* to the "desire of the patriarchs" suggests that he was writing during Advent; his uncertainty about whether Diana knows German shows that they did not as yet know each other well, and the fact that he addresses her as the lady Diana, and his allusions to hills and plains and to the "stronghold," suggest, as we have seen, that she was still at Ronzano, whither she had fled for the second time in November 1222; the supposition that the letter was sent from Würzburg is based on the fact that the manuscript of this particular letter was preserved there.

---

[1] The date and place given to the letters as printed here are taken from the Aron edition, where the probabilities are fully discussed; the same work, and the Altaner edition, may be consulted for the plotting of Jordan's itinerary in general.

[2] [Term used to describe the week beginning with the liturgical feast of Pentecost. *Ed.*]

Jordan was at any rate at Bologna for the next General Chapter, June 1223; and it was then that Diana, with her four companions, was clothed in the habit of the Order. Thereafter Jordan hurried away to preach to the Masters and students of law, who had left Bologna as a result of a quarrel with the commune and had gone to Padua; it seems that in the course of his journey he stopped at Venice, whence he wrote her *Letter 2; Letters 3, 4* and *5* are all from Padua; thence he went to Brescia, and was at Milan by the autumn, and it was probably from this city that he sent *Letter 6.* Pope Honorius III having refused to allow some of the sisters of St. Sixtus' in Rome to go to join the little community at Bologna, Jordan thought of sending some of the nuns from Prouilhe, near Toulouse, the first of all the Dominican monasteries of sisters, and he set off for France, intending to arrange this on his way to Paris; in fact he was delayed at Besançon, partly through illness, partly because of his negotiations with the bishop concerning the foundation of a priory there, and it was probably there that he wrote *Letter 7.*

He seems however to have reached Paris in October or early November; *Letter 8* refers to his preaching to the scholars, which suggests Advent, while the mention of the "city of the saints" suggests All Saints' Day; and he stayed on in Paris (*Letter 9* being also from there) until the General Chapter of Pentecost, 1224.

1

WÜRZBURG (?), DECEMBER 1222

To the Lady Diana, his daughter in loving awe of the Father, his sister by adoption in the Son,[3] his beloved in the love of the Spirit, his companion in the religious life: Brother Jordan, useless servant of the Order of Preachers: health, a swift deliverance from present sorrows, and enjoyment of the joys that are to come.

It was the greatness of your desire which impelled you to write the letter you sent me: let me then tell you a little about the cause of that heavenly desire. Dearest sister, the longing of the patriarchs of old invited Christ, your Bridegroom, God's Son, to suffering; and he came. How then should he not come when your longing invites him to joy?[4] Therefore let all your longing be fixed on heaven. He who would not be bound in hell must bind himself to heavenly things: he who dwells in the plains knows no safety for he is exposed to the attacks of every enemy, but he who is encamped behind the walls and towers of a fortified city, he is secure. You then, beloved, do not pitch your tent in the plains; but as David fled from the face of Saul to the stronghold of Maspha,[5] do you also dwell in desire in the heavenly strongholds.

You do not know German, I think: for indeed you have never been in that country. Those who are of this world speak only the language of this world, for he that is of the earth, of the earth he speaketh.[6] You then, beloved, if you would learn the language of heaven must dwell in heaven by desire: then, when you come back, and read in books or hear from preachers about the things of the spirit, you will understand what they say: for to understand the tongue of the angels you must live in the land of the angels.

There are in man, as you know, two elements, body and soul; and the body is for ever seeking to satisfy its needs in the realm of material things lest it die of hunger: but the soul is more important than the

---

[3] *Rom* 8:15. [Scriptural references are from the Douay (Rheims-Douay) Version. Cross-referencing to the Revised Standard Version is provided in parenthesis. *Ed.*]

[4] i. e. the joy of union with his Mystical Body.

[5] *I Kings* 22:4.   [6] *Jn* 3:31.

body: do not then, beloved, be less concerned for the soul, but on the contrary send it forth sometimes to seek its food in the land of the spirit, that food which is not to be found in the earth and which is bought not with silver but with loving desire.

Who would be so foolish as to allow himself to die for lack of a food which he could have simply by desiring it? Say then with the psalmist: *My eyes are ever towards the Lord,*[7] like the eyes of a poor man looking longingly for an alms from the rich. The bees gather earth's honey from earth's flowers and, careful for their future needs, garner it in their hives: your spirit must die unless it is fed with heavenly honey, for I know that it is of delicate temper and will disdain the nourishment of coarser foods. Send forth your spirit,[8] therefore, beloved, to the flowers of heaven's fields which never fade, that it may draw honey from them and live; and set aside part of what it gathers in the hive of your heart, that if sometimes its desires should languish it may find within itself, in these reserves, a renewal of delight. But you, beloved, when all these desires are fulfilled in you, do not forget the poor man who writes you this letter.

2

VENICE, JULY 1223

Brother Jordan, useless servant of the Order of Preachers, to his dearest daughter in Christ, Sister Diana: on love's way, refreshment as from the rain falling gently upon the earth,[9] and in love's kingdom, the fullness of the torrent of joy.[10]

As you see, by God's good grace I am come safe and sound to Venice, as the Milanese bearer of this letter will be able to tell you in more detail; and now, on the point of departing for Padua, I would urge you to exhort the sisters to pray for me to Jesus Christ, God's Son, that he may give to his voice the voice of power[11] and that my work may produce some fruit to his honour.

---

[7] *Ps* 24(25):15.   [8] *Ps* 103(104):30.   [9] *Ps* 72(73):6.
[10] *Ps* 35:9(36:8).   [11] *Ps* 67:34(68:33).

For the rest, beloved, be strengthened in the Lord and in the might of his power,[12] and give strength to your sisters; and rejoice continually in him in whose right hand are joys that endure for ever.[13] For soon now the time will come for the wedding feast of the Lamb[14] whose right hand is filled with gifts[15] to console those who weep with longing for their true country and to give drink to those whose souls are bitter with the thirst of love: he will wipe away the tearful waters[16] of this present time, and turn their sad insipidity into the wine of the saints, the noble wine which rejoices the heart of man[17] and inebriates with its sweetness the beloved of God, the wine of everlasting gladness, the splendid new wine which at the banqueting table of the court of heaven is poured out for his chosen ones by the Son of God who is blessed for ever and ever. Farewell; and pray for me.

The brothers who are with me, Archangel and John, send you very affectionate greetings. Archangel is very sad that he did not see you before he left Bologna: he fully intended to do so but was hindered by various obstacles. I feel sure that, though he may have seemed negligent in this, he is very fond of you; so forgive him, and keep him in your prayers. Greet the sisters for me. And may the grace of our Lord Jesus Christ be with you.[18]

3

PADUA, JULY 1223

To his beloved daughter in Christ, Diana, at Bologna, brother Jordan, useless servant of the Order of Preachers: everlasting health.

For the time being I cannot be with you to console you, even by letter, as much as I should wish; but I hope that our God, the Paraclete who consoles the humble, will fill you with all his consolation,[19] that consolation which is pure and unalloyed and which pours into the soul the wholeness of truth since he is called, and is, the Spirit of Truth.[20] For

---

[12] *Ephes* 6:10.
[13] *Ps.* 15(16):11.
[14] *Apoc (Rev)* 19:7.
[15] *Ps* 25(26):10.
[16] *Apoc(Rev)* 7:17.
[17] *Ps* 103(104):15.
[18] *Rom* 16:20.
[19] *Acts* 9:31.
[20] *Jn* 15:26.

the moment then find all your support in him; and in him wait patiently for the time of my return: to his care I commend you and all your sisters, my very dear daughters.

I charge both you and them to pray constantly that the Lord be pleased to move the hearts of the scholars at Padua and draw them to himself, for their own souls' sake and for the glory of God and the increase of the Church and of our Order—those among them, that is, whom he knows to be suitable for us. So far we have taken but one; they are all extremely frigid towards us; and if the fire which they lack is to be kindled in them it must be sought elsewhere.

4

PADUA, JULY 1223

Brother Jordan, useless servant of the Order of Preachers, to his beloved sisters in Christ at the convent of St. Agnes: may they be in all things truly God's handmaids.

Keep high festival,[21] and give thanks to the giver of all good things,[22] for the God of mercy and compassion[23] has now been pleased to visit the earth and has plentifully watered it[24]—far more plentifully than we could have hoped. For I had spent a long time preaching to the scholars at Padua, with little or no fruit so far as I could see; wherefore I grew weary and was thinking of leaving: then suddenly the Lord was pleased to move the hearts of many, to pour into them the torrent of his grace, and to give to his voice the voice of power.[25] Now ten have already entered the Order, two of whom are sons of great noblemen of Germany:[26] one of these held high office and had great wealth and

---

[21] *Tobias (Tobit)* 13:10.

[22] A phrase from the *Rule of St. Augustine*, which is also used in the Dominican graces before the evening collation.

[23] *Ps* 85(86):15.   [24] *Ps.* 64(65):10.   [25] *Ps* 67:34(68:33).

[26] One of these was the future St. Albert the Great. At this time he was only sixteen-and-a-half years of age, but was already outstanding because of his exceptional gifts; he had been drawn to the Order but had hesitated for fear of not being able to persevere: with Jordan's help he overcame his scruples once and for all.

many honours; the other also had great revenues, and is truly noble in body and spirit alike. We hope that now many others like these will join: and do you for your part pray fervently to the Lord that he may swiftly turn hope into reality. Farewell.

5

PADUA, AUGUST 1223

Brother Jordan, useless servant of the Order of Preachers, to Diana his beloved sister in Christ: everlasting health.

Have no more anxiety with regard to brother Ventura.[27] I did not call him to Padua to make him prior here. And the prior provincial of the Roman province has written to tell me that all is well at St. Sixtus' and that the sisters are in good heart.

I beg you, of your charity in the Lord, let not your heart be troubled nor let it be afraid[28] if you must suffer tribulation for Christ's sake; for if we are partakers of his sufferings, so shall we be also of his consolations.[29] But let your service of God be a reasonable service,[30] that you may please your invisible Bridegroom. Be strengthened in the Lord:[31] whatever burden he may lay upon you, accept it, and in sorrow be strong to endure, and find patience in your own lowliness. The Lord be with you.

Pray for me, and urge your sisters to pray for me too, that the Lord may bring to completion in us what he has begun.[32] By his grace I have received thirty-three brethren into the Order; apart from two who are not clerics and will become lay brothers, these are all men of hon-

---

[27] The prior provincial of Lombardy, and therefore Diana's superior. Jordan had summoned him to Padua to help with the rapid influx of recruits to the Order and with the founding of a priory there; Diana was troubled at his sudden departure, fearing lest this should mean losing his strong support at a time when the future of St. Agnes' was far from secure. Jordan reassures her; and for her greater comfort adds a guarded reference to the fact that his plans for transferring some of the sisters of St. Sixtus' to Bologna are going well. (Cf. Aron: *Lettres*, p. 9.)

[28] *Jn* 14:27.   [29] *2 Cor* 1:7.   [30] *Rom* 12:1.
[31] *Eph* 6:10.   [32] *2 Cor* 8:6.

ourable standing and sufficient learning; many are of noble rank as you may have learnt from other sources. We expect many more; and six, well suited to us, have already pledged themselves.

Again I say to you: do not be afraid: I will be to you a father, and you shall be to me a daughter[33] and the bride of Christ Jesus; and I will pray to the Lord for you that he may guard and keep you.

6

MILAN, SEPTEMBER 1223

Brother Jordan, useless servant of the Order of Preachers, to Diana, his beloved in Christ: everlasting health.

Since I cannot see you, as I would and as you would, with my bodily eyes, I have written to you a number of times since I left Bologna lest hearing various vague rumours about me you should be troubled in mind. You must know then that at Brescia I was stricken with fever but by the grace of God I recovered my strength and came on to Milan, and I hope in the Lord Jesus that I shall be able to continue my journey. Be consoled therefore in the Lord, that I thereby may be consoled also, for your consolation is a joy and gladness[34] to me before God.

Farewell in the Lord. Greet all the sisters for me, and commend me to their prayers, and bid them also farewell.

---

[33] *2 Kings* 7:14.   [34] *Luke* 1:14.

7

BESANÇON (?), OCTOBER 1223

Brother Jordan, useless servant of the Order of Preachers, to Diana, his beloved sister in Christ and in their common spiritual father [Dominic], his dearest daughter whom the same father left in his care: health, and the consolation of the Holy Spirit.[35]

You have contemned the kingdom of this world and all its pomps[36] for the love of Jesus Christ your beloved Bridegroom; you have chosen and taken to yourself his poverty; so you shall dwell in his courts[37] and be filled with the good things of his house. But what am I saying? Is it really poverty that you have chosen? Rather it is poverty that you have thrown aside and riches that you have chosen; for the poverty of Christ is a willed poverty, that poverty of spirit which gives you the kingdom of heaven. I do not say which *will* give you the kingdom: it gives it you here and now; your Bridegroom himself tells us, Happy are the poor in spirit for theirs *is* the kingdom of heaven.[38] To have the poverty of Christ is to count all the treasures of the world as nothing: is not this then the greatest of all treasures since in comparison with it and because of it all other riches are regarded as worthless and counted as poverty? You are not needy, for you abound in the glory and wealth of his house,[39] you, who have the kingdom of heaven, are not a poor little woman but a queen, the queen of a realm.

Stand then at the right hand of your Bridegroom in vesture of gold,[40] in vesture of love unfeigned,[41] white and ruddy[42] in its ardour and fervour for Christ. And where shall you find the gold wherewith to gild your clothing? Where but in the land of Hevilath,[43] which means

---

[35] *Acts* 9:31.

[36] Responsory ix, in the Dominican Office of Matins, Common of Virgins, [Emmanuel Suarez, O.P., Ed. *Breviarium juxta ritum S. Ordinis Praedicatorum*, (Rome, Santa Sabina, 1952). *Ed.*]

[37] *Ps* 64:5(65:4).   [38] *Mt* 5:3.   [39] *Ps* 111(112):3.

[40] *Ps* 44:10(45:9).   [41] *2 Cor* 6:6.   [42] *Cant(Song)* 5:10.

[43] "And a river went out of the place of pleasure to water paradise, which from thence is divided into four heads. The name of the one is Phison: this is it which compasseth all the land of Hevilath, where gold groweth; and the gold of that land is very good" (*Gen* 2:10-12).

the land of sorrow. In that land is Christ, who calls to us: Attend and see if there be any sorrow like to my sorrow,[44] There you shall find gold; and the gold you shall find in that land is very precious since it is there that Christ shows us the perfection of love, for greater love no man hath than this, that he lay down his life for his friends,[45] as though he should say, See, here is perfect love, here is flawless gold. Here it was that the mines of gold were opened: They have dug my hands and my feet.[46] Others have laboured in these mines: and you, you may enter into their labours and like the bride, the dove, may dwell in the clefts of the rock,[47] and the rock is Christ.[48] There you shall find abundance of gold; there you shall find the fullness of love. And when you have found it shall you not collect it, and so preserve it?

It is the rivers flowing forth from the springs and clefts of the Christ-Rock which proclaim the abundance of this rich red gold, and which indeed are themselves of gold. If then you stand at the King's right hand[49] you will be clothed with the gold that flows from his right side. Therefore approach, stand as close to him as may be, that you may be the more copiously drenched in the gold and that your garments may be made crimson by him who has trodden the winepress.[50] It is there at his right hand that the saints have stood with the queen, their mother the Church, and have washed their robes in the blood of the Lamb.[51] Let this then be the object of all your thought, your care, your toil: for it is here that you will find the gold of the Arabians, that is, of the humble,[52] here you shall be given of the gold of Arabia, which is humility. For this is called the gold of the Arabians or the humble because it is only the humble who can search it out and find it and gather it, since they alone can enter these deep and narrow mines. Be humble and small then in your own eyes; for it is to the little ones that the Lord gives understanding,[53] to the humble that he gives his grace.[54] May he then give you understanding, and instruct you in the way in which you should go, and fix his eyes upon you,[55] for his eyes look upon the poor.[56]

[44] *Lam* 1:12. [45] *Jn* 15:13. [46] *Ps* 21:17(22:16).
[47] *Cant(Song)* 2:14. [48] *1 Cor* 10:4. [49] *Ps* 44:10(45:9).
[50] *Is* 63:3. [51] *Apoc(Rev)* 22:14.
[52] In medieval etymology the name "Araby," meaning plain or lowlands, suggested the idea of humility.
[53] *Ps* 118(119):130. [54] *Jas* 4:6. [55] *Ps* 31(32):8.
[56] *Ps* 10:5(11:4).

Thus briefly have I commended to you poverty, love and humbleness of heart, that by means of these you may come to true riches and joys and honours, through the help of him who is a strong helper,[57] our Lord Jesus Christ who is blessed for ever and ever, Amen.[58]

The prior of Montpellier has written to say that the sisters from Prouilhe will soon be with you.[59] Greet them, and all the other sisters, affectionately for me, and share with them this letter as though it were written for each one of them. Be of good heart in Christ Jesus; and pray devotedly for me.

8

PARIS, OCTOBER-NOVEMBER 1223

Brother Jordan, useless servant of the Order of Preachers, to Diana his beloved sister in Christ: that she may rejoice everlastingly in the joy and the bliss of paradise.

You see, beloved, how with the help of God's grace, and accompanied and followed everywhere by your prayers and those of my [other] daughters I have duly arrived in Paris after a pleasant journey, safe and in good health; and now I hasten to write to you that you may at least have the solace of a greeting by letter since for the time being I cannot console you by being with you and talking with you.

But do you, my daughter, and all the other sisters who are your daughters and mine in the Lord, apply yourselves with all your might, not so much to bodily penances, in which the measure of wisdom and prudence can easily be exceeded, as to the life of virtue and the practice of that godliness which according to the apostle is profitable to all things.[60] Let your hearts be always filled with a burning desire for the blessed city of the saints in paradise, that glorious storeroom of perfect joy and gladness, that abode of light, radiant with the splendour of utter

---

[57] *Ps* 70(71):7.   [58] *2 Cor* 11:31.

[59] Honorius III had refused to allow any of the sisters of St. Sixtus' to go to Bologna; Jordan therefore was now planning to send some from the convent at Prouilhe, St. Dominic's first foundation of nuns.

[60] *1 Tim* 4:8.

beauty, far exceeding the understanding of man: a realm truly divine, worthy to be the dwelling place of him who is created in the image and likeness of God.[61] Let the loving thought of the Bridegroom be constantly in your minds; and as his eyes are upon you, do all you can to make your beauty perfect before him, ridding yourselves of any stain or blemish however small that might sully it and offend his divine gaze. Let there be purity in your hearts and innocence in your lives; in all that you do, be of one mind and one heart, in peace and concord, in unshakeable love, and in that loving humility which is the guardian of all good things; so that, while your souls find deep and lasting delight in the life of holiness, they may themselves be a source of delight to the Son of God who is blessed for ever and ever, Amen.

Pray for me. Give my greetings to your sisters, my beloved daughters in the Lord, and bid them pray for the scholars of Paris, begging the Lord to open their hearts that they may be swiftly converted, while those who have already made good resolutions may faithfully carry them out and so go forward perseveringly to everlasting life.

Farewell. Brother Archangel and brother John salute you. Greet for me your *conversae,* the "familiars" of St. Agnes'[62]—those good ladies who have become its good friends. Be of good heart.

---

[61] *Gen* 1:26.

[62] The term *conversae* is evidently used here to signify, not lay sisters, those members of the community who were mainly concerned with the domestic duties and manual work of the convent, but (as identical with the other term, *familiares,*) women who, without becoming members of the community, but living in or near the convent, helped in its work or towards its support and to some extent shared in its devotional life. The group included Diana's mother and sisters and some of their friends; these were in fact the first women "tertiaries" or members of the Third Order of St. Dominic. (Cf. Aron: *Lettres*, p. 15). [Following the Second Vatican Council's call to remove class distinctions in religious life (*Perfectae Caritatis* 15 [1965]), Dominican monasteries suppressed the category of lay sisters. *Ed.*].

9

PARIS, EASTERTIDE 1224

Brother Jordan, useless servant of the Order of Preachers, to his beloved daughter in Christ, sister Diana, at the convent of St. Agnes: eternal health.

Since I have at the moment a messenger at my disposal, and since I feel that you do want letters from me, I am writing you something forthwith, even though it be only a few words. You must know then that since my arrival in Paris I have been almost all the time in good health except that in the middle of Lent I had a slight attack of tertian fever. As for the scholars at the university, by God's grace things have gone well enough: between Advent and Easter about forty novices joined the Order, of whom many are Masters, others are well-lettered, and of many others again we have high hopes. Thank God then for what we have received, and pray for those whom we still need and hope to receive, that he may work in them both to will and to accomplish, according to his good will.[63]

For yourself, and for your daughters and mine, see to it (as indeed I hope you are doing) that you are all firm in patience, rooted in humility, enlarged in love,[64] and strive always to grow in every virtue that you may go from strength to strength[65] until the Lord of Lords is revealed to you in Sion,[66] in that eternal and abiding Jerusalem where we shall see him as he is,[67] and seeing be filled with unutterable joy, a joy no man can take from us.[68]

Farewell in Christ. Greet all my daughters for me. Brother John salutes you.

---

[63] *Phil* 2:13.   [64] *2 Cor* 6:13.   [65] *Ps* 83:8(84:7).
[66] Ibid.   [67] *1 Jn* 3:2.   [68] *Jn* 16:22.

January 1225 to October 1225

A FTER the General Chapter of 1224 at Paris, Jordan started off on his usual journey back to Bologna, to be there in time for his customary Lenten course of sermons; the normal winter route would be by way of the Rhône valley and the Corniche, and Jordan would doubtless visit the new priories in France and Provence on his way. *Letter 10* seems to date from early 1225; and the fact that the provincial of Provence is with him, and that the setting up of the priory at Avignon took some time, suggests that it was written from there. Meanwhile Honorius III, at the instigation of Jordan's friend Cardinal Ugolino, had given way over the sisters of St. Sixtus,' so that the Prouilhe scheme was no longer necessary, but Jordan merely mentions the fact in his letter as he would soon be able to explain everything fully by word of mouth.

His great friend Henry of Cologne was with him at the Chapter of 1225 at Bologna, and thereafter accompanied him to Germany where he wished to visit the priories; the route would presumably be through Lombardy, the valley of the Adige, and across the Brenner Pass; the references in *Letter 11* to the breviary Office of Virgin Saints and to "entering into the joy" of the Order, and the mention in *Letter 12* of Jordana and Mary, novices recently entered (the fact that the latter is called "our" Mary connects her with Henry, who was writing with Jordan, and who had presumably therefore brought her with them to Bologna), would allude to their clothing or taking of vows in the Order; as this was due to take place soon after the Chapter it is probable that Jordan was still in Italy, though on his way to the Alps. It is likely then that the first of the two letters was written at some early stop such as Modena or Mantua; the mention of the buying of cloth for a habit in the second letter suggests Verona since the nearby market-town of Cologna was noted for its woolen goods. *Letters 13, 14* follow on quickly: the preceding one had gone by a special messenger, brother Bernard the German, doubtless chosen by Jordan as being an old friend and therefore a great comfort both to Diana and to her family: he must have returned quickly with disturbing news of Diana's distress and also of that tendency to an excessive and dangerous austerity against which Jordan so often warns her.

These two letters date from the summer of 1225, and Jordan was in fact delayed in Verona by sickness until the middle of August. But then, as he describes in *Letter 15*, he was able to set out again, though worried about the political troubles in Italy and the consequent danger to St. Agnes' which stood in a very vulnerable spot outside the city walls; he writes this letter from Trent, where he is able to preach to the people, that is, in German (he would address his University audiences in Latin); then he goes on to Magdeburg *(Letter 16,* September) and, doubtless after other stops on the way, arrives at Cologne in October. Henry had left him at some point on their journey and had gone on ahead; when Jordan arrives it is to find Henry gravely ill, and *Letter 17* describes his grief at his death.[1]

[1] Cf. also Appendix, pp. 123 ff.

10

AVIGNON (?), JANUARY 1225

Brother Jordan, useless servant of the Order of Preachers, to his beloved daughter in Christ, sister Diana, and to the whole Chapter of the sisters at St. Agnes' in Bologna: that in the choir of the holy virgins they may follow the Lamb, the Virgin's Son, whithersoever he goeth.²

For the moment I write to you only briefly, for I hope by God's gift to be able very soon to talk with you. But meanwhile, beloved daughters, do you each and all in your prayers to God beg him to give me his good grace, unhappy sinner that I am, that in the might of that grace prevenient and supporting I may be able to carry out all his will in the ministry he has entrusted to me. For I have great trust in your prayers, especially when you all invoke him with one mind and one heart, for it can hardly be that when many pray together some should not be heard.

If any unwonted temptations come upon you, do not be affrighted: these are the wars and seditions³ against which the Lord would have his servants and handmaids to be strong and great of heart, since he himself, whose battle you fight, is your helper. For indeed what prince, seeing his tender little handmaidens or his own sisters fighting against a cruel enemy because of him and on his behalf would not at once arise, especially if he himself were mighty in battle,⁴ provided they did not take to flight at the time of attack but turned to entreat the face of their lord.⁵ Fight therefore not only manfully but prudently; for as Solomon tells us, war is managed with due ordering,⁶ and you will fight with prudence if you set out to subdue your carnal nature not precipitately but little by little, advancing by measured steps in the way of the virtues, not trying to fly but climbing cautiously up the scale of perfection till at length you come to the summit of all perfection.⁷

And, briefly to conclude; in all things you should observe due measure, that you may act always with moderation; for only the love of God knows neither measure nor moderation. And that love is nourished not

---

² *Apoc (Rev)* 14:4.   ³ *Lk* 21:9.   ⁴ *Ps* 23(24):8.
⁵ *3 Kings(1 Kings)* 13:6.   ⁶ *Prov* 24:6.   ⁷ *Ps* 118(119):96.

by the afflicting of the flesh but by holy desires and loving contemplation and through the cherishing of that sisterly love whereby each of
you loves the others as herself. Farewell.

As for the sisters of Prouilhe, this does not seem an opportune
moment for me to send any of them to you; but I will explain all this to
you by word of mouth when I see you.

Brother Bertrand, the prior provincial [of Provence] salutes you all.

11

MODENA OR MANTUA (?), JUNE 1225

*Brother Jordan, useless servant of the Order of Preachers, to his
beloved daughters at St. Agnes,' the brides of the Lamb: that they
may follow the Lamb whithersoever he goeth.*[8]

My daughters are decked out and adorned indeed,[9] but not like those
daughters of men of whom the psalmist speaks who are adorned round
about after the similitude of a temple and in whom in truth there is the
similitude but not the sanctitude. The temple of God is holy, and you are
that temple,[10] nor is there any doubt but that the Lord is in his holy temple,[11] dwelling within you. Weep not then, daughters of Jerusalem,[12]
weep not for yourselves because in the body I am far from you, but
rejoice in the presence of your Bridegroom who is in the midst of you.
And indeed I too am present to you in spirit,[13] happy in the thought that
yet a little while and my daughters shall be brought to the King our
Lord, shall be brought to him with gladness and rejoicing.[14] They shall
be brought after her who is the queen, after Mary, the chosen one, his
Maiden-Mother, she alone his dove, his beautiful one, she who is all fair
and there is no blemish in her.[15] This is she that never knew bed of
shame,[16] she that is full of charity and love, full of grace, she that is
blessed among women and the Lord is with her.[17] After her shall the

---

[8] *Apoc (Rev)* 14:4.   [9] *Ps* 143(144):12.   [10] *1 Cor* 3:16.
[11] *Ps* 10:5(11:4).   [12] *Lk* 23:28.   [13] *1 Cor* 5:3
[14] *Ps* 44:14(45:13) ff.   [15] *Cant(Song)* 2:10; 4:7.   [16] *Wis* 3:13.
[17] *Lk* 1:28.

brides of Christ be brought into the temple of the King[18] that temple which is not made with hands,[19] and there, as Isaiah said, the bridegroom shall rejoice over the bride and your God shall rejoice over you.[20]

You shall come into Sion with praise, and everlasting joy shall be upon your heads[21]–that everlasting crown which is called joy because it is the fullness of all bliss. You shall receive a kingdom of glory and a crown of beauty at the hand of the Lord,[22] for it is then that he will say to his faithful servant, Enter thou into the joy of thy Lord[23]–the joy of that lord to whom in particular you have sworn fealty, the Order of Preachers; and so all your sorrow shall be turned into joy, and your joy no man shall take from you.[24] we shall rejoice everlastingly with Christ Jesus who is blessed for ever and ever, Amen.[25]

Farewell. Rejoice always in the Lord; and pray for me and for the whole Order.

12

VERONA, JUNE, 1225

Brother Jordan, useless servant of the Order of Preachers, to his beloved daughter in Christ, Diana: health, gladness in the grace of the Holy Spirit,[26] and unending joy in his consolations.[27]

I feel that you are very sad; but your sorrow shall be turned into joy,[28] for according to the multitude of the sorrows in your heart the consolations of the Lord will give joy to you, and the Paraclete, whom the Father will send to you,[29] will console you. I am sending brother Bernard to you, that he may be a comfort both to you and to the Lady Jacobina; and I beg and beseech him who consoles his own in all their sorrows[30] that he may solace the heaviness of your hearts. For now, as we read in *Peter,[31]* we must for a little time be made sorrowful that in somewhat we may be made like to him who said, My soul is sorrowful

---

[18] *Ps* 44:15(45:14).	[19] *Acts* 17:24.	[20] *Is* 62:5.
[21] *Is* 35:10.	[22] *Wis.* 5:17.	[23] *Mt* 25:21.
[24] *Jn* 26:20, 22.	[25] *Rom* 9:5.	[26] *Lk* 10:21.
[27] Collect of the *Mass of the Holy Spirit.*		[28] *Jn* 16:20
[29] *Jn* 14:26.	[30] *2 Cor* 1:4.	[31] *1 Pet* 1:6.

even unto death.[32] But after death we are to rejoice and make merry, for so we read that the just feast and rejoice before God,[33] and sorrow and weeping are no more. And if you feel that your sorrow is perhaps a little excessive, then must you cry with the psalmist: Why art thou sad, O my soul, and why dost thou disquiet me? hope in God.[34] Your brother has been snatched away; but it was lest wickedness should mar his understanding, or the deceits of this world should beguile his soul.[35] Do not then let your sadness be excessive, my dearest ones, like those others who have no hope:[36] your hope should be filled full of the immortality which is in you, and so you should beg the Lord to grant you joy of heart.

Greet for me the Lady Otta, your mother, and your sister Otta too, and the Lady Jacobina, and all the sisters at St. Agnes' who are so dear to me in the Lord. Fare you well.

Your brother Henry greets you very affectionately and sends you his deep sympathy in your sorrow. The Lord, who brings the calm after the storm, will give serenity back to your souls, will turn the storm into a gentle breeze and bring you to the haven of perfect tranquility of will.[37] Farewell. Greet for me Jordana and our Mary: with Master Jordan's permission I am sending Jordana some cloth to be made into a tunic and capuce,[38] hoping that this can be done. Farewell.

13

VERONA, JUNE 1225

Brother Jordan, useless servant of the Order of Preachers, to his beloved daughter in Christ, Diana: everlasting health and joy in the consolation of the Holy Spirit.[39]

You must know, beloved, that as the Scripture says, through many tribulations we must enter into the kingdom of God[40] but when we

[32] *Mt* 26:38. [33] *Ps* 67:4(68:3). [34] *Ps* 42:5(43:4).
[35] *Wis* 4:11. [36] *1 Thess* 4:12. [37] *Ps* 106(107):29 ff.
[38] This, in the primitive Order, was a garment comprising both scapular and hood.
[39] *Acts* 9:31. [40] *Acts* 14:21.

have reached the kingdom we shall know sorrow no more; meanwhile your Bridegroom Christ Jesus will never desert you, for he hath said, I will not leave thee neither will I forsake thee;[41] and this is true even though sometimes he may seem to be gone far from you so that you cry, Why, O Lord, hast thou retired afar off? why dost thou slight me *in opportunitatibus,*[42] in times of want and weakness when help is needed and opportune? And when do we most need help if not, as the psalmist goes on to say, in time of trouble?[43] But certainly he will not then forsake you, he will draw nearer to you, for the Lord is nigh unto them that are troubled in heart.[44] If then sometimes you are sad and go sorrowful whilst the enemy afflicteth you,[45] think of the words of your Bridegroom who is the joy of angels, My soul is sorrowful even unto death;[46] if pain afflict you, remember those other words, Attend and see if there be any pain like to my pain;[47] for indeed he alone hath eyes for misery and sorrow.[48]

After labour there is rest for us; after suffering, everlasting consolation: according to the great multitude of our sorrows his comfort will rejoice our souls by his own gift who is your Bridegroom, who with his Father is blessed for ever, Amen.

Do not abstain too much from food and drink and sleep; but in all things be moderate and patient.

Greet for me all the sisters, and the Lady Otta your mother, and your sister Otta, and Jacobina. It gives me joy to know that you were not too deeply distressed by your brother's death. See to it that your sisters do not give themselves excessively to penitential practices but proceed in all things with due order. I have written you this letter with my own hand. Fare well in Christ; and pray for me.

I, brother Henry, salute you Diana with all my heart.

---

[41] *Heb* 13:5. [42] *Ps* 9b(10):1. [43] Ibid.
[44] *Ps* 33:19(34:18). [45] *Ps* 42(43):2. [46] *Mt* 26:38.
[47] *Lam* 1:12. [48] *Ps* 9b(10):14.

14

VERONA, JUNE 1225

Brother Jordan, useless servant of the Order of Preachers, to his beloved daughter in Christ, Diana, and all the convent of St. Agnes: health, and the consolation of the Spirit.

Since it is the great office of godliness to offer spiritual solace to those who are in tribulation,[49] I beg you of your charity to do everything in your power to console the Lady Jacobina in her bereavement; thus you will please God yourselves and may also win her soul to him.

Give yourself zealously to prayer; and pray for me, for brother Henry the prior of Cologne, and for brother Bernard and my other companions on my journeyings, that the Lord may direct our ways according to his good pleasure and may grant us by his grace to win salvation for souls: it is for this that we have set ourselves to work, and by your prayers you will be sharers in the work.

Farewell; and may the only begotten Son of God who is in the bosom of the Father[50] come into your hearts and make his abode there daily with you,[51] Amen.

Greet for me the Lady Otta, and Otta your sister, as also Jacobina and Agnes.[52]

15

TRENT, AUGUST 1225

Brother Jordan, useless servant of the Order of Preachers, to his beloved daughter in Christ, sister Diana: everlasting health.

I do not requite your love fully; of that I am deeply convinced: you love me more than I love you. But I cannot bear you to be so afflicted

---

[49] Cf. *Jas* 1:27.   [50] *Jn* 1:18.   [51] *Jn* 14:23.
[52] This Agnes was probably a relative, perhaps the mother or sister, of Jacobina visiting her in her bereavement; cf. Aron, *Lettres*, p. 112.

in body and distressed in mind by reason of this love of yours which is so precious to me: and I have indeed heard that you are too oppressed and troubled because of my illness, you and your sisters too. In fact, however, your prayer has entered into the sight of the Lord,[53] and in his mercy he has accorded me a further span of life, or rather a time for repentance. On the feast of the blessed Laurence, though I was still rather weak, I left Verona, on the advice of the doctor, and had gained much strength by the time I arrived here at Trent, so that I was able to preach to the people on the feast of Our Lady's Assumption into heaven and on the next day to the scholars. But I am anxious about you and about your sisters; anxious to know what things are against you,[54] Beloved daughter, be constant and trust in the Lord:[55] no matter what trials vex you, what difficulties beset you on every side, God is in the midst of you all[56] and therefore you must not be disquieted. Fare you well in Christ. This letter I write you from Trent, the day after the feast of the Assumption.

16

MAGDEBURG, SEPTEMBER 1225

Brother Jordan, useless servant of the Order of Preachers, to his beloved daughter Diana: may she be brought by Jesus Christ her Bridegroom into his cellar of wine.[57]

Since I know that your love makes you anxious about me I wanted to let you know that after leaving Verona, the God of our salvation making my journey prosperous for me[58] and giving new strength to my weak body, on the third day after the feast of St. Matthew I arrived here at Magdeburg safe and in good health and was given a very joyful welcome by our brethren, who had long been anxious about me, and by a great number of other people. I was much consoled to find everything in our convent here in good order, and the recent reception of several novices rejoiced me greatly. Give thanks then to God, whose

---

53 *Ps* 87:3(88:2).   54 *Rom* 8:31.   55 *Dan* 23:35
56 *Mt* 18:20.   57 *Cant(Song)* 2:4.   58 *Ps* 67:20(68:19).

mercy looks so kindly upon us in all things,[59] and gives us so much more than we deserve.

For the rest, beloved, preserve a due measure in your labours and apply the curb of discretion to all that you do; so that as you run after your Bridegroom, drawn by the fragrance of his ointments[60] and longing to offer him myrrh, which is the chastening of the flesh, you may yet leave place for an offering of gold, following the example of the three holy Wise Men who, opening their treasure-chests, offered to Jesus gold, frankincense and myrrh.[61] Thus your treasure chest must not be so filled with myrrh as to leave no room for the gold of wisdom and discretion. You must be able to say with the bride in the *Song of Songs,* A bundle of myrrh is my beloved to me;[62] she does not liken her beloved to a great weight or load of myrrh but to a little bundle, as showing that a due measure is to be observed in all things. Often I have told you this when I was with you, and now that I am far away I say it again: you must go forward on your way with such prudence as to be able to climb up, without stumbling, to your goal which is the land of heaven, led thither by the Son of God, Christ Jesus, who is blessed for ever and ever,[63] Amen.

Commend me to the prayers of your sisters and greet them for me; and may the Spirit of truth be with you in all things.[64]

17

COLOGNE, OCTOBER 1225

Brother Jordan, useless servant of the Order of Preachers, to his beloved bride and daughter in Jesus Christ, Diana, and to the holy congregation of St. Agnes': may you have that everlasting salvation which hath appeared to all men,[65] and may you follow the Lamb whithersoever he goeth.[66]

When God wipes away all tears from the eyes of the saints[67] he will wipe away those torrents of tears which you shed, weeping so bitterly,

---

[59] *Ps.* 68:17 (69:16). [60] *Cant(Song)* 1:3. [61] *Mt* 2:11.
[62] *Cant(Song)* 1:12. [63] *2 Cor* 11:31. [64] *Jn* 15:26
[65] *Titus* 2:11. [66] *Apoc(Rev)* 14:4. [67] *Apoc(Rev)* 21:4.

as I left you. For my part I had hoped to be able, under the inspiration of the gentle Consoling Spirit, to send back to you by letter some few words of comfort even though this could not be according to the measure of the multitude of sorrows in your heart;[68] but my hope has been made vain, for all comfort is hidden from my heart:[69] he who divides to everyone—and divides one from another—according as he will,[70] he will not in time to come make a separation between brothers,[71] he has already made it, according to his good pleasure, and so is it done.[72] Wherefore I have wept, and still sometimes now I weep. I weep for my most faithful companion, my sweetest friend, I weep for the brother who loved me so much, I weep for my dearest son, Henry, the prior of Cologne. He indeed has gone, happily, to his Father, to dwell in his Fatherland; but me he has left, unhappy, in this present wicked world.[73]

Nor was it I alone who wept for him: the whole of Cologne was filled with lamentation. Never was such sorrow seen for a man. Especially bitter was the mourning among the brethren and the holy widows and virgins,[74] for indeed he was a lover of the brethren, and from his very childhood had been filled with an ardent love of chastity. He was a godly man, wise, humble of heart, modest, sober, chaste and peace-loving,[75] living while yet on this earth the life of the angels.

Now, as I firmly believe, he reigns with God and the Lamb of God, he reigns with Christ, a precious jewel among preachers. Being made perfect in a short space, he fulfilled a long time,[76] and he has heard that sweet commendation, Well done, thou good and faithful servant, enter thou into the joy of thy Lord.[77] He is not lost to us, he is but gone before us: he has passed from darkness to the light of the everlasting glory,[78] from danger to security, from penury to riches, from strife to victory, from sorrow to joy, from time to eternity, from the stench of a sinful world to the sweet fragrance of that life which abides for ever.

Let us then follow him, eager to enter in our turn into that everlasting rest. But remember that you are not to be too hasty, for you have

---

[68] *Ps* 93(94):19.   [69] *Osee(Hos)* 13:14.   [70] *1 Cor* 12:11.
[71] *Osee(Hos)* 13:15.   [72] *Job* 1:21.   [73] *Gal* 1:4.
[74] The Béguines, who made a vow of chastity and lived under the spiritual direction of the friars; cf. Aron, *Lettres*, p. 37.
[75] Vespers hymn of the Office of Confessors.   [76] *Wis* 4:13.
[77] *Mt* 25:21.   [78] *Wis* 10:14.

yet a great way to go.[79] If you become weary, remember how Jesus your Lord was wearied with his journey and so, being weary, sat down by the well.[80] If you feel heavy of heart, listless, weak, cry to him who exults as a giant to run his course:[81] Draw me after thee, we will run to follow thee, drawn by the fragrance of thy ointments.[82] But in all things be humble and patient, as he looks to you to be: behold, patiently the husbandman brings forth the precious fruit of the earth,[83] and in like manner you, not laying waste your flesh but tilling and tending your hearts, must wait patiently for the precious and blessed fruit of the glorious Virgin Mary's womb.

And you, dearest Diana, my daughter, try not to be overwhelmed with sorrow because of your brother or of your sister Otta,[84] your dear, gentle, faithful friend whom I would so much have wished to see if your Lord Jesus had but willed it. Find comfort in the only begotten Son of God, your Bridegroom, in whose presence we shall again see our friends, and in whom and before whom we shall rejoice, as they that rejoice in the harvest.[85] If now we must be for a little time made sorrowful,[86] if going we must weep as we scatter the seed, yet, in the harvest time, coming we shall come with joyfulness carrying our sheaves,[87] and in Christ Jesus we shall rejoice with joy unspeakable[88] and all our sorrow shall be turned into joy and our joy no man shall take from us:[89] to which may the same Christ Jesus your Bridegroom lead us, who with the Father and the Holy Spirit reigns for ever and ever, Amen.

Fare you well in Christ. Diana, greet my Lady Otta for me, and tell her that I would fain be with her beloved Otta and my beloved Henry. O Diana, how much happier they are, these two, than you and I! They are in glory, we in wretchedness; theirs is the victory, we must yet do battle; we are still in exile, they have come home. Yet let us pray for them, so that if in death they were still burdened with some small failings they may be the more swiftly loosed therefrom and receive their crowns.

---

[79] *3 Kings (1 Kings)* 19:7.   [80] *Jn* 4:6.   [81] *Ps* 18:6(19:5).

[82] *Cant (Song)* 1:3.   [83] *Jas* 5:7.

[84] Whose death therefore must have occurred soon after that of her brother Brancaleone. It seems that in the four years 1225 to 1229 Diana lost in turn, brother, sister, mother, and finally father (cf. Aron, *Lettres*, p. 112).

[85] *Is* 9:3.   [86] *1 Pet* 1:6.   [87] *Ps* 125(126):5–7.

[88] *1 Pet* 1:8.   [89] *Jn* 16:20, 22.

As for me, I am well enough in bodily health and I have hope that Christ will keep my soul safe and will keep us both in his Spirit, Amen.

Brother Conrad, who was with us at Bologna, greets you and begs you to pray for him.

March 1226 to June 1227

B Y the spring of 1226 Jordan is in Paris again; the twenty-one novices mentioned in *Letter 18* were received into the Order there in February, as we know from other sources; he remained in Paris, first to preach the Lenten sermons to the University and then for the General Chapter in June; *Letter 19* seems to have been sent from there some time during the summer.

When he writes *Letter 20* he is once again on the road since he expresses his hope of seeing Diana again soon; his reference to the dangers still besetting the convent imply that the truce with the Emperor (January, 1227) had not yet been concluded; the fact that brother Conrad the German is with him, and that the priory at Vienna was established in 1226, may lead us to suppose that he travelled by way of Germany and the Austrian Tyrol, and that perhaps this letter was written from Vienna itself.

It seems likely that on his arrival in Italy Jordan went straight to Rome and obtained from the Pope the Bull (December 1226) committing the convent of St. Agnes to the care of the Order; and that he went thence to Bologna, taking with him from St. Sixtus' the sister, Cecilia Cesarini, who was to be prioress of St. Agnes' and who is first mentioned in *Letter 21*. His stay in Bologna would have been short, however, as the scholars had not yet returned and he would have gone on to other university cities in northern Italy; but he returned, probably for Lent, certainly for the Chapter at Whitsuntide. At this Chapter the Bull just mentioned was promulgated; *Letter 22* evidently refers to this fact and its concluding sentences imply that Jordan is in northern Italy; *Letter 23* seems to be from the same region but states Jordan's intention of setting off for Rome: Honorius III had died in the spring and the new Pope, Gregory IX, was Jordan's old friend Ugolino, who granted him various privileges in Bulls dated July 1227: it is likely therefore that this letter was written a few weeks earlier, probably in June.

18

PARIS, MARCH 1226

Brother Jordan, useless servant of the Order of Preachers, to his beloved daughter Diana: health in him who is the Saviour of all.[1]

We have just heard of the troubles and distresses which afflict Bologna and therefore yourself and your sisters;[2] and my grief is the greater inasmuch as I know I cannot in this matter give you any counsel or comfort except in so far as you can be helped by my prayers, sinner that I am, and by the prayers of our brethren, which I hope may be fruitful in the sight of God who is not wont to reject the prayers of his servants in their time of need nor be deaf to their supplications. Be not affrighted therefore, beloved, nor lose heart, whatever trouble may befall; for you have a Bridegroom tried and tempered by all sorrows so that he knows how to compassionate with all sorrows, especially yours and those of his other brides. For he is a God jealous in his love,[3] and he will send his angel[4] to you who with jealous care will guard your body from harm, and still more your spirit.

Be nothing solicitous[5] therefore, my daughter, but take courage and be valiant;[6] for your Bridegroom is Emmanuel, God-with-us, who does not forsake those who trust in him but is with them as he promised even to the consummation of the world.[7] Be tranquil then, casting all your care upon him[8] whose power never can be vanquished, whose wisdom is never at fault, whose loving-kindness never wearies. Such is your beloved, who has the power and wisdom and will to set you free from all troubles and distresses. Think then, in the meantime, upon him, who gave himself, not his brothers and sisters, to the onslaught of wickedness; and so you will not grow faint in soul.

The Emperor has no respect for men of religion, nor will he listen to them: on the contrary, as he himself says, it is painful for him even to

---

[1] *1 Tim* 4:10.
[2] The re-forming of the Lombard League in 1226 had made the plight of the cities of northern Italy more critical than ever.
[3] *Ex* 20:5.   [4] *Mal* 3:1.   [5] *Phil* 4:6.
[6] *Deut* 31:7.   [7] *Mt* 28:20.   [8] *1 Pet* 5:7.

see them. As you said in your letter to me....[9] I am profoundly convinced that in these circumstances my presence would be of no avail at all, and so for the moment I do not come to you; but if the Lord is willing I shall come later on this year and then we shall see each other again and our hearts shall rejoice.[10] In this present life joy and sorrow succeed one another; but yet a little while and the hour will come when our joy will be full and it shall never be taken from us.[11]

And I would not have you ignorant,[12] beloved, of the favour which the Lord has shown to the Order and of how the brethren grow in numbers and in merit. Since our arrival at Paris twenty-one novices have entered in the space of four weeks; six of these are Masters of Arts and others are Bachelors, able men and well-suited to the work of the Order. And the Lord Bishop of Paris is so well disposed to our brethren that he came in person to have speech with us and ate with the community in the refectory; the Lord Cardinal Legate of France also ate with the brothers in the refectory on the feast of the Annunciation; finally, the Queen[13] herself holds our brotherhood in tender affection, and talked with me personally and in private about her affairs. All this I tell you, my daughter, that you may praise and glorify our Lord for giving us these and other blessings and also that you may cause your sisters also, as is meet and just, to give thanks unceasingly. Farewell. Have prayers offered for me and for the brethren.

Brother Conrad the German, who was with me at Bologna, salutes you and begs for prayers for himself. Farewell again.

---

[9] The rest of the sentence is lacking. [10] *Jn* 26:22.
[11] *Jn* 26:19, 24; *Lk* 10:42. [12] *1 Thess* 4:12.
[13] Blanche of Castille (1185?–1252), queen of Louis VIII of France.

19

PARIS, SUMMER 1226

To his beloved daughters in Christ, the sisters of St. Agnes' at Bologna, brother Jordan, useless servant of the Order of Preachers, everlasting life and joy in the Lamb whom they follow.

Beloved daughters, though you run after your Bridegroom, drawn by the fragrance of his ointments,[14] see to it that you tread circumspectly,[15] that you so run that you may obtain the prize,[16] being neither laggard and slow to run nor so hasty that your feet stumble[17] and you fail to reach your goal. Narrow and strait indeed is the way that leadeth to life;[18] so you must go forward warily lest you stray from it to the one side through lack of diligence and fervour or to the other side through excessive austerity. In your case it is the second of the two dangers that I fear the more: I fear lest, unwisely chastising your flesh, you should fall into worse calamity and find yourselves hindered in the way of the Lord, the way leading to that city which is your home,[19] the city of the Lord of hosts which God hath founded for ever.[20]

The foundations of this city are in the holy mountains,[21] or rather mountain, of the Lord, the mountain which his right hand hath purchased[22] that is, his Son who is the right hand of God the Father; for it is on him that its foundations rest, and the Highest himself hath founded it.[23] O heavenly city, carefree dwelling place, home of every joy; O city of God, glorious things are said of thee,[24] whose people live without murmuring, tranquil and content, wanting for nothing. The way to this city is indeed hazardous; but when it shall be given to us to reach the blessed Jerusalem which is built as a city, then there will be no more dangers to fear: nothing there to bring about ruin, but only eternal peace, eternal stability, eternal security; for does not the Spirit say of the saints who dwell in the city, From henceforth now they may rest from their labours?[25] Meanwhile, for as long as we must toil along the

---

[14] *Cant(Song)* 1:4

[17] *Prov* 19:2.

[20] *Ps* 47:9(48:8).

[23] *Ps* 86(87):5.

[15] *Eph* 5:15.

[18] *Mt* 7:14.

[21] *Ps* 86(87):1.

[24] *Ps* 86(87):3.

[16] *1 Cor* 9:24

[19] *Ps* 106(107):7.

[22] *Ps* 77(78):54.

[25] *Apoc(Rev)* 14:3.

road let us go forward not with unwise impetuosity but with prudence, until we come to the city, under the leadership of our Lord Jesus Christ who is blessed above all things for ever and ever, Amen.

Beloved daughters, if any trouble or sorrow come upon you, bear all with patience and evenness of temper, awaiting the time when for small troubles endured you shall be given great glory, for sorrow joy, for mourning everlasting comfort.

Fare you well; and pray for me even as I have you daily in my prayers, begging the Father of mercies and God of all consolation[26] that he will give you all a heart to worship him and to do his will.[27]

The grace of our Lord Jesus Christ be with your spirit, Amen.[28]

20

VIENNA (?), SUMMER 1226

Brother Jordan, useless servant of the Order of Preachers, to his beloved daughters, brides of Jesus Christ, Diana and the other sisters at St. Agnes': joy and the consolation of the Holy Spirit.

Be strengthened, beloved daughters, in the Lord Jesus[29] your Bridegroom whom you have wisely chosen above all the desirable things of this world, and whom, as I hope, you hold fast in the strong embrace of your prayers and tears lest he depart from you. Be not afraid therefore; for now no judgment stands against you[30] since you have your Lord, the author of your salvation,[31] who has the will and wisdom and power to free you from every distress and affliction and anguish of heart.[32] Henceforth then, if any one of you be for a time cast down with weariness of spirit or afflicted with aridity of heart so that the torrent of devoted love seems to be dried up, will she dare to cry, My Lord hath forsaken me[33] and hath no care for me, since the feelings of joy and devotion I have hitherto known are now gone from me? Such things must never be uttered by a bride of the gentle Christ Jesus:

---

[26] *2 Cor* 1:3. [27] *2 Mach (Macc)* 1:3. [28] *Gal* 6:18
[29] *Eph* 6:10. [30] *Rom* 8:1. [31] *Heb* 2:10.
[32] *2 Cor* 2:4. [33] *Is* 49:14.

let them speak thus who know not his ways nor how, as I so often told you when I was with you, he is wont to kindle the love of his brides: how for a time he will draw away from you that you may seek him with greater ardour, and having sought may find him with greater joy, and having found may hold him with greater love, and having held may never let him go; like the bride in the *Song of Songs* who, after long searchings and questionings whether any had seen her beloved, at length when she had found him exclaimed, I have held him and I will not let him go.[34]

And be comforted, you his brides, by the sweet words wherewith he answered one of his brides of whom Isaiah tells us, who was bewailing her dereliction; for Isaiah writes that Sion said, The Lord hath forsaken me and the Lord hath forgotten me;[35] now the name Sion means a mirror, and signifies the holy soul who frequently gazes into the mirror which is Christ, the unspotted mirror of God's majesty.[36] This soul, seeing and feeling sometimes her own hardness of heart, cries out: The Lord hath forsaken me and the Lord hath forgotten me; but hear now what the Lord replies to her: Can a woman forget her infant, so as not to have pity on the son of her womb? and if she should forget, yet will not I forget thee; for behold, I have graven thy image in the palms of my hands.[37]

May you have these words often in your minds; for then, I think, no matter what trouble or distress or even long-continuing aridity of heart should come upon you, you would not readily hearken to the devil's suggestion that the Lord had forsaken you. For thus says the blessed Bernard: No matter how cruelly you be afflicted, think not that you are forsaken, but remember that it is written: I am with him in tribulation, I will deliver him and I will glorify him.[38]

For the rest, I commend myself to your prayers. I hope that with God's help I may soon see you and console you in the Lord. Farewell. Brother Conrad, who was with us at Bologna, greets you and commends himself to your prayers.

---

[34] *Cant (Song)* 3:4.   [35] *Is* 49:14.   [36] *Wis* 7:26.   [37] *Is* 49:4.
[38] *Ps* 90(91):15; cf. St. Bernard of Clairvaux, *Sermo 16, 17 in Ps. xc.*

21

NORTHERN ITALY, JANUARY 1227

Brother Jordan, useless servant of the Order of Preachers, to Diana, his dearest daughter in Christ: health, and the consolation of the Holy Spirit[39] wherewith he has consoled the hearts of the children of God.

I know well how, as we learn from the holy prophets of old and again in these latter days from Paul through whom Christ hath spoken to us,[40] we should rejoice with the servants of the Lord Jesus, and particularly in their own consolation and joy. Wherefore, having just had news of the consolation wherewith you and your sisters have been consoled by the favour you have now been granted,[41] I rejoice with you all, whose joy is my own.

Beloved daughter, you know that hitherto I have always and in every place been with you, desiring and seeking your good and that of all your sisters; but now, for the future, I shall with God's grace be yet more solicitous for you. I commit to your care the letter which the Sovereign Pontiff entrusted to me for you: guard it well.

And, lest I seem ungrateful, I would have you know of the wonderful mercies which our Saviour has shown forth to me[42] since I left you;[43] for he has brought to our Order eighteen suitable candidates, and there are others who are resolved to join: pray for all these, therefore, and give thanks often to Christ for his gifts to me.

Greet the prioress for me, and Jordana and all the sisters.

---

[39] *Acts* 9:31.　　[40] *Heb* 1:2.　　[41] Cf. *supra*, p. 75.　　[42] *Ps* 16(17):7.

[43] Jordan had perhaps been briefly in Bologna for the conclusion of the truce between the Lombard cities and the Emperor; if on his return from Germany he had gone first to Rome he may have brought with him to Bologna Cecilia Cesarini, from St. Sixtus,' and installed her as prioress—now mentioned for the first time in this letter (Cf. Aron, *Lettres*, p. 49).

22

NORTHERN ITALY, JUNE 1227

Brother Jordan, useless servant of the Order of Preachers, to his beloved daughter in Christ, Diana: eternal health.

You tell me in your letter that you did not wish to die and enter into your Father's house where there are many mansions[44] until the convent of St. Agnes had been fully established and confirmed under the jurisdiction of the Order, but that now this is done you feel more carefree, and long to be dissolved and be with Christ.[45] Certainly I want you to have this longing in your inmost heart; but I would not have you try to hasten its fulfilment by scrupulous searchings of conscience or immoderate bodily disciplines, for as Solomon tells us, he that is hasty, his feet shall stumble.[46] Take care then not to run with so much haste that you grow faint in the way: as the apostle says, you must so run, in so well ordered a manner, that you may obtain the prize.[47]

And may the blessed God be pleased so to draw us after him that we may be able the more sweetly and gaily to run after him, drawn by the fragrance of his ointments:[48] may he lead us by a way of his own choosing and take us to himself at last in glory,[49] and so in glory we shall appear with him,[50] thanks to his Son Jesus Christ, your Bridegroom, glorious and ever to be praised, who rules over all things, blessed for ever, Amen.[51]

I am sending you the little girl on whose behalf I appealed to your kindness: have care of her, as indeed I know you will. I am afraid this may be a burden to you; but they would not care for her or see to her upbringing and so I felt a great pity for her, for the love of him who suffered for our salvation. I should be glad if one of the Germans among our brethren could talk to her once or if possible twice a week lest she should forget that language which she knows as well as the tongue of Lombardy. Will you then tell the prior of our convent to send someone; and make her talk to him, for she is reluctant now to talk German, hav-

---

[44] *Jn* 14:2.   [45] *Phil* 1:23.   [46] *Prov* 19:2.
[47] *1 Cor* 9:24.   [48] *Cant(Song)* 1:3.   [49] *Ps* 72(73):24.
[50] *Col* 3:4.   [51] *Rom* 9:5.

ing since Easter been with the Lord Gerard where she heard nothing but the Lombard language spoken. But he says she is a good child, and is sorry to lose her.

Farewell in Christ.

23

NORTHERN ITALY, JUNE 1227

Brother Jordan, useless servant of the Order of Preachers, to his beloved Diana, handmaid of St. Agnes: eternal health.

The Lord who made me;[52] and has so often made me his beneficiary, has now through his Son Jesus Christ again and again multiplied his mercy in me,[53] to his honour and glory and the good of souls, for in the might of the Holy Spirit he has brought to our Order about thirty novices, well versed in letters and well suited to us: for which do you and all the sisters give thanks to God.

For yourselves, be strengthened in the Lord Jesus Christ, and may he dwell always in your hearts.[54] For a heart empty of Christ is like a husk empty of grain: borne away on the winds, blown this way and that by temptation; whereas the grain of corn, even though the wind blow, will not be carried away by it, since it has weight, and in the same way the heart in which Christ dwells is made firm, so that though temptation beat down on it and buffet it, still it will not be swept hither and thither or be blown away. Say then, and say in your hearts: Let others cling to whom they will, as for me, it is good for me to cling to my God;[55] and again: My soul hath clung close to thee.[56] The chaff is swept away by the wind because it does not cling strongly to the grain: that we may cling strongly to him, he has bound us to himself, fast knit in his love, as he says by the mouth of the prophet, I have bound close to me all the house of Israel,[57] that is to say, the hearts of those who see God, who keep the Lord always in their sight.[58] As then he has willed

---

[52] *Ps* 94(95):6. [53] *Ps* 35:8(36:7). [54] *Eph* 6:10; 3:17.
[55] *Ps* 72(73):28. [56] *Ps* 62:9(63:8). [57] *Jer* 13:11.
[58] *Ps* 15(16):8.

to join us to himself, so may he deign to draw us after him and to lead us to life everlasting, he who is blessed for ever and ever, Amen.

I am setting off now for Rome. Pray for me. You may read this letter to all the sisters.

Christmastide 1227 to April 1231

E VENTS were now moving fast, both in the Order and in the world at large. The Order was growing rapidly, thanks mainly to the preaching and influence of Jordan himself: "It is an established fact and worthy of all belief," says the thirteenth-century *Lives of the Brethren,* "that since the rise of the religious Orders no one ever drew so many men of letters and clerics of note to any Order as [Jordan] did to the Order of Preachers."[1] Influence and opportunity marched with numerical growth. Jordan was the Pope's personal friend, he was well received by princes, the bishop of Paris was extremely friendly to the Order; the crusade was being preached, Frederick preparing to set off for the Holy Land, the war with the Albigenses was approaching its climax and the count of Toulouse was soon to submit to France and to the Church. Jordan thought it wise to convoke a *Capitulum Generalissimum* to meet in Paris in 1228, and himself set out for that city. He arrived in December; *Letters 24, 25* were written from there, the first soon after Christmas, the second probably about the time of the Chapter. Diana's father died early in 1229; Jordan heard the news, and wrote *Letter 26,* at Milan on his way back to Bologna to preach the Lent there and attend the Chapter; the Chapter over, he was soon on the road again, going by way of the university cities of northern Italy *(Letters 27, 28)* to embark at Genoa *(Letter 29* and the letter to Stephen, Appendix, *Letter 1)* for Provence, the Order having been offered the new chair of theology at Toulouse. Thence he would go on through Languedoc, Switzerland (the priory at Zurich was established in this year) and part of Germany and Burgundy to Paris where he arrived in October. *Letter 30* was sent from there; *Letter 31* was clearly written about Christmas time but it is impossible to say where; in January 1230, however, Jordan is in England, and he stayed there several months *(Letter 32),* preaching the Lent at Oxford, and returning to Paris in time for the Chapter at Whitsun. *Letter 33* seems to have been written as he was on the point of leaving there and setting off once again on the journey to Bologna, per-

[1] *Lives of the Brethren,* Pt. IV, ch.10.

haps towards the end of 1230; he preached the Lent in Padua, and wrote thence in Easter week to the priory of St. Jacques in Paris (Appendix, *Letter 6); Letter 34* to Diana was clearly written at the same time.

24

PARIS, CHRISTMASTIDE 1227

Brother Jordan, useless servant of the Order of Preachers, to his beloved daughter in Christ, sister Diana: health, and the fullness of the embrace of Christ Jesus.

Since it is not given to me, my beloved, to see you with my bodily eyes as often as you would wish and I would wish, nor to find comfort in your presence, my heart finds some slight solace, and a tempering of its longing, when I can visit you by letter and tell you how things are with me; at the same time I would gladly hear more frequently how you are faring, for your progress in the way of the Lord, and that of the other sisters, is a joy to me. I could indeed have written to you some while since, had it not been for lack of a messenger. But now I must tell you that fifteen days before Christmas, the God of our salvation having made our journey prosperous to us,[2] I arrived safely at our convent in Paris and I am there still, preaching and awaiting the accustomed mercy of our God. Do you therefore, and the sisters who are with you, be constant and earnest in prayer that God may hearken to the desire of his poor[3] and in his goodness may gently and effectively touch the hearts of the scholars at the university here, and increase our numbers.

But this messenger is in haste to be gone, so I must write to you more at length, if God permits me, another time. For the moment I simply bid you have in mind what I have so often urged on you and others: that your first concern must be to take prudent care of yourself, lest through weariness of spirit or weakness of body you should deprive your body of the fruit of its good works, your soul of its devotion, your neighbour of a good example, and God of his honour, not to speak of other evils which are wont to spring from the vice of imprudence.

You have sometimes learnt of this by experience also; so I would have you most cautious and heedful for the other sisters; for, as I have often warned you, bodily exercise is profitable to little,[4] and in vigils and fastings and tears the due measure is easily exceeded; but virtue—

[2] *Ps* 67:20(68:19).   [3] *Ps* 9b(10):17.   [4] *1 Tim* 4:8.

humility and patience, kindness and obedience, charity also and sobriety—can never grow to excess. In these then I encourage you, that you may abound the more,[5] for while I have confidence in the Lord that you will abound in all these things, still nothing in this life is so perfect that it cannot become more perfect, till happily we come to that place where there is no longer any possibility of deficiency, where all are filled with such perfection that they cannot want for more, where all sufficiency will be from God[6] and, most abundantly of all, will be God himself who will be all in all,[7] worthy of praise and glorious for ever and ever,[8] Amen.

25

PARIS (?), SPRING 1228 (?)

To Diana his dear daughter, or rather his beloved sister, in Christ, brother Jordan, useless servant of the Order of Preachers: eternal health in Christ Jesus our Saviour.

Beloved, I can write to you only very hurriedly; yet I had to try to write you something, however brief, in the hope of giving you if I can a little joy. You are so deeply engraven on my heart that the more I realize how truly you love me from the depths of your soul, the more incapable I am of forgetting you and the more constantly you are in my thoughts; for your love of me moves me deeply and makes my love for you burn more strongly.

I must end this letter abruptly; but may he who is the supreme Consoler and Paraclete, the Spirit of Truth, possess and comfort your heart; and may he grant us to be with one another for ever in the heavenly Jerusalem, through the grace of our Lord Jesus Christ who rules over all things, blessed for ever, Amen.[9]

Farewell, beloved, and pray for me often and earnestly to the Lord: I am much in need of prayer because of my many faults, and I pray but

---

[5] *1 Thess* 4:1.   [6] *2 Cor* 3:5.   [7] *1 Cor* 15:28.
[8] *Dan* 3:56.   [9] *Rom* 9:5.

seldom myself:[10] do you therefore exhort your sisters that they too may make good my deficiencies in this respect.

26

MILAN, SPRING 1229

Brother Jordan, useless servant of the Order of Preachers, to Diana his beloved daughter in Christ: eternal health.

Those who are left to live on in this world weep and are sad for the death of their friends who go before them; but those who have died first do not mourn in the other world over the death of those who come after them. And you, beloved, you are long since dead with Christ if your life is hid with him in glory;[11] therefore you have long since gone before your father into death and so you should not grieve for him, for if you do you must think of yourself as not yet fully dead with Christ, If I say this, it is not that your father's death, of which I have just heard here in Milan, does not affect me: it does indeed, though principally on your account. But think with wonder of the gentleness of God, how he takes from you your parents according to the flesh, in this transitory life, only that he himself may be your friend according to the spirit, through life everlasting: he takes from you what you could not hope to cling to for ever, only to give you what is eternal and shall never be taken from you for ever. Amen.

I write you this from Milan, very briefly since the messenger cannot wait. Farewell, and greet all your sisters for me. Soon, if God wills, I shall see you all.

---

[10] It is reasonable to interpret this as referring to the very heavy pressure of work with which Jordan was burdened at the time, perhaps combined with the self-depreciation of a holy and humble man. The *Lives of the Brethren* tells us of him that "God was pleased to bestow on him a very special gift of prayer, which neither his anxiety for his brethren's welfare, nor his long journeyings, nor any kind of occupation, could ever shorten" (Pt. IV, chap. 6).

[11] *Col* 3:3.

27

PADUA, JUNE-JULY 1229

Brother Jordan of the Order of Preachers, to his beloved daughters in Christ, the sisters of St. Agnes' at Bologna: may they seek and obtain Christ Jesus.

The thought of you all rejoices my heart, beloved daughters, since I know how eagerly, in unity together, you walk with the Lord, seeking nothing save him in whom alone is your sufficiency and without whom all possessions must be not wealth but penury. And him you possess the more completely, the more completely you give yourselves to him, withdrawing yourselves in body and mind alike from this present wicked world[12] so as to belong to your Bridegroom alone who alone redeems all, and to be, as the apostle says, holy both in body and in spirit.[13] And indeed it is quite certain that God gives himself to us the more abundantly in so far as we are the more generous in giving ourselves to him.

Wherefore, since I know well your eagerness[14] for all things, and how you have not only relinquished for the love of Christ Jesus, the Bridegroom of your souls, whatever you could relinquish for his sake, but also labour faithfully day by day in such wise as to be able always more and more to empty yourselves[15] and to cast your care upon the Lord,[16] clinging only to the love of your Redeemer to whom it is good for you to cling[17]—knowing all this, with joy in my heart I give thanks to him who called you unto his grace wherein.[18] See to it then, my dearest daughters, that you receive not this grace in vain,[19] this matchless boon which is his gift, the perfect gift which took not its beginning from you but is from above, coming down from the Father of all light,[20] who through his grace hath shined in your hearts,[21] calling you into his marvellous light.[22] Therefore, whilst you have the light, walk in the light, that the darkness overtake you not:[23] walk in the light of your God.

[12] *Gal* 1:4. [13] *1 Cor* 7:34. [14] *2 Cor* 9:2.
[15] *Phil* 2:7. [16] *Ps* 54:23(55:22). [17] *Ps* 72(73):28.
[18] *Phil* 2:13. [19] *2 Cor* 6:1. [20] *Jas* 1:17.
[21] *2 Cor* 4:6. [22] *1 Pet* 2:9. [23] *Jn* 12:35.

He who walks goes forward with moderation: he does not wander aimlessly, through negligence; nor does he rush on headlong with imprudent rashness and impetuosity. This latter evil is certainly the one I fear most for you: that some among you may indeed run without prudence or moderation, with excessive shedding of tears, immoderate vigils, fastings, or other similar austerities ill-fitted to your feeble strength of body, for indeed you are not as robust as you would like to think, and one or other of you might easily be in reality completely exhausted even while thinking she still had great reserves of strength. I have often, as you know, warned you of this, for it is this that I always fear for you; and so I do not hesitate to warn you again, for to write the same thing again to you is indeed not wearisome to me and is necessary for you.[24] Be very cautious therefore in this matter.

For the rest, as previously you prayed to the Lord concerning the scholars at Padua and your prayers were heard, for twenty or more good, sound men have entered the Order, so now you must take care to offer him abundant thanks, while at the same time in no wise desisting from your petitions.

May the grace of our Lord Jesus Christ be with you, Amen.[25] Brother Gerard, my companion on my journey, salutes you all in Christ Jesus.

28

MILAN, JULY 1229

Brother Jordan, useless servant of the Order of Preachers, to his beloved daughter in God's Son Jesus Christ, sister Diana at Bologna: health, and fullness of joy in the embrace of Christ Jesus.

I know that you are anxious about me, as I am about you, in the Lord; and therefore I want to tell you briefly my news. After my arrival at Vercelli the Lord brought us a number of good men of high academic standing: three Germans, the most distinguished of those now in the city; four excellent men from Provence; and three or four good

---

[24] *Phil* 3:1.   [25] *Rom* 16:20.

Lombards; all of these entered the Order within a short space of time. Give thanks to God, then, with your sisters, for he never for a moment forgets to show forth his mercy to us.

For the rest, I am, thank God, in good health. Let it not be a heavy burden on you, beloved, that I cannot all the time be with you in the flesh, for in spirit I am always with you in love unalloyed. Yet I cannot wonder that you are sad when I am far from you since, do what I may, I myself cannot but be sad that you are far from me; but I console myself with the thought that this separation will not last for ever: soon it will be over, soon we shall be able to see one another, endlessly, in the presence of God's Son Jesus Christ who is blessed for ever, Amen.

Greet the prioress for me, and all the sisters, my beloved daughters, especially the novice Galiana. Pray for me.

29

GENOA, AUGUST 1229

To his most loving daughter in Jesus Christ, sister Diana at Bologna, brother Jordan, useless servant of the Order of Preachers: health and the grace of the Lord her Bridegroom.

I see from your letter that you are troubled about this new Constitution;[26] but I think you have been misled by an imprudent interpretation of it and that your fears are groundless, for neither I nor the diffinitors[27] [at the Chapter] ever meant it to apply to our own sisters: we never so understood it, and indeed the idea never entered our heads; I am quite certain of this, for I was present at all the meetings of the Chapter and of the diffinitors, and know the reasons for all the legislation that has been passed up to the present time. The new Constitution has nothing to do with our own sisters; the reason for it

---

[26] Cf. *supra*, pp. 20-22.

[27] ["Diffinitors are friars elected by the members of the provinces to represent them to a general chapter. They are a separate body from the elected superiors." (Brunetta, "The Canonical Status of Persons, Structures, and Relationships in the Order of Preachers: An Historical-Juridical Study," p. 225, n. 1). *Ed.*]

was simply that in various provinces our brethren have got into the way of too readily allowing women outside the Order, for their spiritual advancement, to receive the habit and tonsure[28] or to make a vow of chastity. Do not discuss this new law, therefore, with anyone at any time; but have no anxiety about it, no harm can come to you from it; and whoever put these doubts into your mind acted very indiscreetly, trying to alarm you when there was no cause for alarm.

For the rest, my beloved, be in all things confident and joyful; and what is lacking to you because I cannot be with you, make up for in the company of a better friend, your Bridegroom Jesus Christ whom you may have more constantly with you in spirit and in truth,[29] and who speaks to you more sweetly and to better purpose, than Jordan. And if sometimes he seems to turn his face away from you and become a stranger to you, you must see this not as a punishment but as a grace. He is the bond whereby we are bound together; in him my spirit is fast knit with your spirit; in him you are always without ceasing present to me wherever I may wander: he who is your Bridegroom, Jesus Christ God's Son, to whom is honour and empire everlasting, Amen.[30] Fare well in the Lord; and greet my daughters for me.

This same day on which I write to you I am to leave Genoa. I am in good health.

Those sisters who ought to have taken their vows by now may safely do so in the hands of the prioress or of the prior of our convent there or of the provincial acting in my name; and this will give me as much joy as if they were making their profession in my own hands, nor must they ever feel any misgiving about this procedure.

---

[28] A sacred rite of initiation into the clerical or monastic state by shaving the head. In the context of the nuns, this meant the cutting of the young woman's hair when she was received as a novice.

[29] *Jn* 4:23.   [30] *1 Tim* 6:16.

30

PARIS, OCTOBER 1229

Brother Jordan, useless servant of the Order of Preachers, to his beloved daughters in Jesus Christ, the sisters of St. Agnes': that they may attain to Jesus whom they follow.

As I know that you are often anxious at heart about me, I write to tell you that by the help of your prayers, and the Lord making my journey prosperous for me,[31] I travelled safely from Lombardy through Provence, Auvergne, Burgundy and France and so arrived at Paris, where I write this letter to you after the feast of the blessed Denis. Everywhere I found the brethren increasing in numbers and making good progress, through God's grace, for which cause I give thanks to God the giver of all good things.[32]

But I exhort you, beloved daughters, that with earnest prayer you beseech God the author of peace to grant unity in his peace to the holy Church; for throughout the world wars and seditions[33] rage, putting many souls in peril of eternal damnation; and do you, dear daughters, knowing this, burn the more ardently with love of your Bridegroom who has snatched you from the turmoil of the world and established you in his peace, established you so firmly that even though trouble or distress come upon you from without, the peace within you should rather be increased than diminished, so long as you are patient in all things.

And indeed there is nothing that can come upon you whether of good or of adverse fortune that you should not learn to accept with tranquil mind, fixing your hearts on the Lord by whose unfailing help we can make light of prosperity and be fearless in the face of adversity. I hope that you abound in all good things from the Lord;[34] and may he from whose hands these gifts come to you be pleased to preserve them and cause them ever to increase in richness within you, he your Bridegroom Jesus Christ, God's Son, to whom is honour and empire everlasting,[35] Amen.

[31] *Ps* 67:20(68:19).   [32] Cf. *supra*, p. 54, n. 22.   [33] *Lk* 21:9.
[34] *2 Cor* 9:8.   [35] *1 Tim.*6:16.

Farewell, all of you, dear to me in the Lord; and pray for me.
I, brother Gerard, greet you all fondly, and commend myself to your prayers.

31

FRANCE, CHRISTMASTIDE 1229

Brother Jordan, useless servant of the Order of Preachers, to his beloved daughter in Christ, sister Diana in the convent of St. Agnes at Bologna: may she be filled with richness of heavenly gifts.[36]

I cannot find the time to write you the long letter your love would wish for and I would so gladly send; none the less I do write, I send you a very little word, the Word made little in the crib,[37] the Word who was made flesh for us, the Word of salvation and grace, of sweetness and glory, the Word who is good and gentle, Jesus Christ, and him crucified,[38] Christ raised up on the cross, raised in praise to the Father's right hand: to whom and in whom do you raise up your soul and find there your rest unending for ever and ever.[39] Read over this Word in your heart, turn it over in your mind, let it be sweet as honey on your lips; ponder it, dwell on it, that it may dwell with you and in you for ever.

There is another word that I send you, small and brief: my love, which will speak for me to your love in your heart and will content it. May this word too be yours, and likewise dwell with you for ever.

Farewell, and pray for me.

---

[36] *Ps* 147:14.

[37] An echo of St. Bernard of Clairvaux's *Sermo I in Vigilia Natalis Domini: "Jesus Christus Filius Dei nascitur in Bethleem Jude. O breve verbum de verbo abbreviato"*; which itself echoes *Rom* 9:28 and *Is* 10:22.

[38] *1 Cor* 2:1.   [39] *Ps* 131(132):14.

32

ENGLAND, JANUARY 1230

To his beloved daughters in Christ Jesus, the sisters of St. Agnes' at Bologna, brother Jordan, useless servant of the Order of Preachers: health, and may they attain to the Bridegroom whom they follow.

Short is our way, small our task, but infinite the repose to which, my daughters, dearest of all to me, we hasten; let us then rejoice and exult to run our course,[40] that we may make the Lord's covenants the subject of our song while we are yet in the body, exiled from the Lord's presence in the place of our pilgrimage.[41] These things I write to you in order that, if some tide of tribulation should sweep over the soul of any one of you, she may be able to support it with patience and indeed with joy.

For it is through tribulations that we lay up to ourselves treasure in heaven,[42] so that when the day comes wherein our sorrow shall be turned into joy,[43] the consolations that are given us will be measured according to the multitude of our present sorrows.[44] Moreover, by an inner process of refining, tribulation makes the soul itself more pure, so that it is more on its guard against the manifold daily wiles of the enemy and at the same time is more richly filled with divine consolation. Wherefore, if tribulation is bitter it is none the less good and desirable, for it produces patience,[45] it tests and proves the mind, it gives understanding to those whom it tries, it brings an increase of spiritual solace and lays up a copious treasure of heavenly joy for the future; whence the Lord says to those who suffer affliction, Be glad in that day and rejoice, for behold, your reward is great in heaven.[46]

But, dearest daughters, while you thus trample under foot all alien enticements for the love of your Bridegroom, and freely accept and triumphantly endure what is painful and hard to bear, you must at the same time labour diligently to keep to the middle of your way and beware lest in anything you exceed, having always in mind the warning

---

[40] *Ps* 18:6(19:5). [41] *Ps* 118(119):54; *2 Cor* 5:6.
[42] *Mt* 6:20. [43] *Jn* 16:20. [44] *Ps* 93(94):19.
[45] *Rom* 5:3. [46] *Lk* 6:23.

of the sage that he that is hasty, his feet shall stumble.[47] Many times I have admonished you about this, by word of mouth when with you, by letter when absent, that you might sedulously avoid any indiscreet excess of austerity; wherefore if any one of you should still, after receiving so many warnings, imprudently fall into such excess she would be all the more guilty of negligence.

For the rest, I have hope that by the grace of Christ Jesus you walk always in holiness: instant in prayer, assiduous in contemplation, prompt to obey, eager to labour, slow to speak,[48] constant in keeping the silence, clothing yourselves in tender compassion, kindness, humility, patience, gentleness, charity;[49] wherefore I feel confident that so far as you are concerned there is no need for me to urge such matters on you at length; I should rather give thanks always to my God for you, for the grace of God that is given you in Christ Jesus,[50] God's Son and your Bridegroom, to whom is honour and glory, power and empire for ever and ever, Amen.[51]

Fare you well always in Christ Jesus. I write to you from England, in good health, before the feast of the Purification of the Blessed Virgin. Pray for me without ceasing unto the Lord,[52] that he may always open wide his hands to us and may direct his word, through our lips, to his own honour and to the good of the Church and the increase of our Order. At the University of Oxford, where I am at present, the Lord has given us great hopes of a good catch:[53] beg him frequently that in those especially whom we hope to catch, as in others also, his will may be accomplished.

Brother Gerard greets you, and commends himself earnestly to your prayers.

---

[47] *Prov* 19:2.
[48] *Jas* 1:19.
[49] *Col* 3:12.
[50] *1 Cor* 1:4.
[51] *Apoc(Rev)* 7:12.
[52] *Acts* 12:5.
[53] *Lk* 5:5, 9.

33

(?), DECEMBER 1230

To his beloved daughters in the Son of God, the sisters of St. Agnes' at Bologna, brother Jordan, useless servant of the Order of Preachers: health, and abundance of the joys which are in Christ Jesus our Lord.

The words spoken by the friend of the Bridegroom are very different from those of the Bridegroom himself.[54] You, beloved daughters, have heard the gentle whisper of your Bridegroom himself and you rejoice with joy because of his voice;[55] wherefore what I write to you must be of little moment, I who, though I seem to be the Bridegroom's friend, am less even than that.

Still, as I do fulfil that office, since he has charged me to be your bridesman;[56] as I am jealous on your behalf with the jealousy of God himself; as I have betrothed you to Christ that no other but he should claim you;[57] so I charge you to show yourselves worthy of his embrace, adorning the bridal chamber of your hearts to receive Christ the King who greatly desires your beauty[58] and strewing his nuptial bed with flowers[59] in purity of heart and goodness of conscience and faith unfeigned.[60]

Now these flowers are the virtues: humility is a goodly flower, patience is good, obedience is good, kindness is good, gentleness is good, all other such virtues are good: but greater than these is charity.[61] Often and gladly will the Bridegroom come to the bridal chamber of the heart which he finds strewn with these flowers and bedecked with these ornaments; wherefore, my most dear daughters in Christ, do you study to acquire these virtuous qualities, for this is that godliness which is profitable to all things, whereas bodily exercise is profitable to little.[62]

---

[54] *Jn* 3:29, 30.   [55] Ibid.
[56] The *paranymphos*, whose office it was to fetch the bride from her house and lead her to the bridegroom.
[57] *2 Cor* 11:2.   [58] *Ps* 44:12(45:11).   [59] *Cant(Song)* 1:15.
[60] *1 Tim* 1:5.   [61] *Col* 3:12; *1 Cor* 13:13.   [62] *1 Tim* 4:8.

For as I have often warned you and shall warn you again: in vigils, in fastings, in tears too, it is easy to fall into excess; but virtue can never grow to excess. I have confidence indeed in the Lord Jesus Christ that you do abound in all these qualities; none the less I exhort you that you may abound the more.[63] For there is nothing in this life so perfect that it cannot be made more perfect, until we come to that place where nothing defective can find entry, where each of us will be filled with a perfection so great that he can want for nothing further, where no indigence will find room, for God himself will be superabundant plenitude to all things, he who is glorious and worthy to be praised for ever and ever, Amen.[64]

Farewell, beloved daughters, and pray for me, that swiftly and safely God may bring me to you. Give abundant thanks to God for the many great men and sound scholars whom he has given to our Order this year. Brother Gerard salutes you and commends himself to your prayers.

34

PADUA, APRIL 1231

To Diana, his beloved daughter in the Son of God, brother Jordan, useless servant of the Order of Preachers: everlasting health.

Your petitions and those of your sisters have been made known to God[65] to no small purpose, for he has given us some thirty novices, good men of high birth and sound scholarship, several of them Masters. Master James, the archdeacon[66] of Ravenna and provost of Bobbio, who before his entry into the Order was offered a bishopric but refused it and who is the best professor of law in Lombardy, took the habit and made his profession on the Wednesday before Easter Day; with him there entered also another archdeacon, a fine young man, from one of the noblest and wealthiest families of Hungary. In the same

---

[63] *1 Thess* 4:1.   [64] *Dan* 3:56.   [65] *Phil* 4:6.

[66] [Priests who exercised important ecclesiastical administration in the service of their bishop. The category is now defunct. *Ed.*]

way elsewhere throughout the world, as I am often informed, our brethren are multiplied and grow both in number,[67] since for one brother whom perhaps we have left in the world we now receive more than a hundred, and better ones.

Yet mark well how in the Gospel, when the Lord promised that he would render an hundredfold, he added, But with tribulations;[68] wherefore we must never for a moment allow ourselves to forget that if we would receive an hundredfold we must be prepared equally to suffer tribulation. Yet shall the time come when the Lord shall repay us no longer an hundredfold but with infinitude, when no tribulation shall any longer come to you, but together we shall drink of the pure and unmixed chalice of everlasting joy. Meanwhile we must wait patiently, accepting comfort with humility and tribulation with courage, and finding both the comfort and the strength in God's Son Jesus Christ, who rules over all things, blessed for ever and ever, Amen.[69]

I would write to you often were it not that so often I lack either the leisure or else a messenger. Farewell; and greet our daughters for me. Soon, if the Lord grant it, we shall be able to console one another. Meanwhile brother Henry, the prior provincial from across the seas,[70] will take my place and console you for the time being in my stead.

I, brother Gerard, your son, salute you.

[67] *Mt* 19:29.   [68] *Mk* 10:30.   [69] *Rom* 9:5.
[70] i.e. the Holy Land.

May 1231 to 1236

THE Chapter of 1231 took place in May; soon afterwards Jordan is again touring northern Italy: Modena, Reggio, Vercelli, Milan. Evidently he did not think when he left Bologna that his absence would be a long one, and so took no formal leave of Diana; but later he decided that he must press on if he were to cross the Alps before winter; in fact he was detained a long time at Milan by recurrent bouts of fever, and was still there in the spring of 1232 *(Letters 35-41)*. Diana had hoped that he would not leave Italy without seeing her *(Letter 41)* and perhaps in view of his weakness would give up the attempt to get to Paris for the Chapter; but he was determined to try, and set off, only to suffer a relapse at Trent *(Letter 42)* and be laid up there for several months, so that he was unable in fact to be at the Chapter.

We do not know where *Letter 43* was written, but the references to his health and his hope of seeing her soon suggest that it dates from the autumn or early winter of 1232; by Advent of that year he is back at Padua *(Letter 44);* he preached the Lent of 1233 in northern Italy, and *Letter 45* with its Passiontide[1] imagery was sent from there; in May he is back at Bologna for the Chapter, and then seems to have set off on a long journey, though where it took him is not clear. At any rate it seems likely that *Letter 46,* in which he tells Diana of his dream about her, was written in the course of it, perhaps in the spring of 1234. Altaner thinks that he was ill at Zurich in June and July, thus missing the Chapter at Paris; certainly he was in Strasbourg in early August, as *Letter 47,* probably written from there, makes clear, and was able to celebrate there the canonization of St. Dominic; but judging by *Letter 48,* sent from Paris early in 1235, he had been unable to get to Bologna in 1234, doubtless through further illness, and had spent all the winter in Paris; now, as he wrote, he was planning to be at Bologna soon, but again his hopes were frustrated: illness, and the loss of one of his eyes, kept him in France and caused him to miss the Chapter at Bologna.

---

[1] [The two weeks between Passion (Palm) Sunday and Easter. *Ed.*]

He had not been back there since 1233; he was never, it seems, to see Diana again in this life. The mention in *Letter* 49 of "the ends of the earth" may suggest that he was planning a lengthy journey; the phrase is repeated in the final letter, written in the course of the journey though we do not know when and where. The *Capitulum Generalissimum* of 1236 was held in Paris; and it seems that Jordan set sail soon afterwards for the Holy Land. His intention was to return in time to preach the Lent to the University of Naples, and he embarked at Acre for the return voyage in February 1237, but his ship was wrecked off the Syrian coast.

The papal penitentiaries, brothers Godfrey and Reginald, wrote to the community of St. Jacques: "Learn that a great storm arose at sea, which dashed to pieces on the beach the vessel in which our sweet Father and Master was sailing, and he with his two companions and twenty-nine other persons were drowned."[2] His body was taken back to Acre and buried there; "and there the blessed father lies bestowing benefits on many."[3] Diana had preceded him; for according to the archives of St. Agnes' she died after being thirteen years in the Order, that is to say in the course of 1236. They had reached, almost together, those "shining mansions" of which they had so often thought, and for which they had so greatly longed.

[2] Cf. *Lives of the Brethren*, Pt. IV, ch. 25.   [3] Ibid.

35

MODENA, MAY 1231

To his beloved daughter Diana, brother Jordan, useless servant of the Order of Preachers, health and consolation in Christ Jesus.

When I have to part from you I do so with heavy heart; yet you add sorrow to my sorrow since I see you then so inconsolably weighed down that I cannot but be saddened not only by our separation which afflicts us both but also by your own desolation as well. Why are you thus anguished? Am I not yours, am I not with you: yours in labour, yours in rest; yours when I am with you, yours when I am far away; yours in prayer, yours in merit, yours too, as I hope, in the eternal reward? What would you do if I were to die? Certainly not even for my death should you weep so inconsolably. For were I to die you would not be losing me: you would be sending me before you to those shining dwellings [which God has established],[4] that I abiding there might pray for you to the Father and so be of much greater use to you there, living with the Lord, than here in this world where I die all the day long. Be comforted then, and so act the more manfully, and be refreshed in the mercy and grace of your Lord Christ Jesus, who is blessed for ever, Amen.

Farewell; and greet the sisters for me, especially the prioress, and Galiana, Juliet, Cardiana; and any other of our friends whom you know. Christ Jesus be with you, Amen.

---

[4] Cf. Responsory. vii in the Dominican Office of Matins for feasts of martyrs: "All round about thee, O Lord, is the light that never faileth, where thou hast established shining dwellings: there shall the souls of the saints find rest." [Emmanuel Suarez, O.P., Ed. *Breviarium juxta ritum S. Ordinis Praedicatorum*, (Rome, Santa Sabina, 1952). *Ed.*]

36

REGGIO (?), JULY 1231

Brother Jordan, useless servant of the Order of Preachers, to his beloved daughter Diana and his other daughters of St. Agnes': eternal health.

I stayed a week at Modena, labouring much in sowing but, for my sins, reaping little; for which cause I left there and came on to Reggio, and am planning to continue my journey in short stages, going from convent to convent, till I come to the mountains;[5] for after careful consideration I decided I must cross them before the winter. This means that I cannot very well return to Bologna; and so I must beg you, of your love for me, to be patient with me for thus continuing my journey and to forgive me for not having expressly taken leave of you as I usually do: I acted thus in order to spare both you and myself; for I could not have borne without grieving the sight of your many bitter tears, while on the other hand, being uncertain about my plans, I was afraid that you would be grieved if I spoke of them.

Now therefore I beg of you, as you love me, that you be not sorrowful,[6] so that I too may be of good heart; rather rejoice in your Bridegroom Jesus Christ who is in your midst: he will console you, through his Holy Spirit who is called the Paraclete or Comforter; so that, according to the multitude of the sorrows of your hearts[7]—which now for a little time you must bear because of the divers temptations and tribulations of this present life—his consolations may rejoice your souls, till being strengthened by them and as it were drawn on by the fragrance of his ointments[8] you come to him your Saviour in whom you shall obtain joy and gladness, and all sorrows and mourning shall flee away.[9] So shall we be filled with the good things of his house,[10] and dwelling therein with his blessed, his chosen ones, shall praise him for ever and ever,[11] Amen.

---

[5] i.e. the Alps; cf. *supra,* p. 101.   [6] *1 Thess* 6:12.   [7] *Ps* 93(94):19.
[8] *Cant(Song)* 1:3.   [9] *Is* 35:10.   [10] *Ps* 64:5(65:4).
[11] *Ps* 83:5(84:4).

37

VERCELLI, JULY 1231

Brother Jordan, useless servant of the Order of Preachers, to Diana, his beloved daughter in Jesus: health, and the grace of spiritual joys.

Since I left you, a short time ago, God has been with us and has prospered us continually. You have already heard, I think, about those who entered the Order at Reggio: do not forget to thank God for them. I wrote to you when I reached Vercelli: we received there only a single novice, but one of good character and attainments, and I hope that soon by God's grace we shall have more. Brother Henry from across the seas is very dangerously ill; and I earnestly commend him to you and the other sisters, that you pray faithfully to the Lord for him for we fear that he is beyond doubt lost to us.

For the rest, beloved, cast your care upon the Lord;[12] find comfort always in him, and in him learn how to triumph over whatever adversities this mutable life may bring you. Do not be anxious about me; for he who has care of you in Bologna will also, I trust, have care of me on my various journeyings, since your remaining in the quietude of your convent and my divers wanderings in the world are equally done only for the love of him. He is our sole end: he who both guides us in our present exile and will be our reward in heaven, he who is blessed for ever and ever, Amen.

Farewell in Christ Jesus; and greet for me all my beloved daughters, especially the prioress, Galiana, Jordana and Juliet.

Your son Gerard sends you and them tender greetings. Commend us to their prayers.

---

[12] Ps 54:23 (55:23).

38

MILAN, AUGUST 1231

Brother Jordan, useless servant of the Order of Preachers, to his beloved daughter in Jesus Christ, sister Diana: health, and the consolation of the Holy Spirit the Paraclete.

You will have heard, beloved, of how, as I was returning from Vercelli to Milan with eight novices,[13] good men and well-suited to our Order, and was proposing to go on thence into Germany, I was stricken down with a tertian fever; I have had three attacks as I write this, and expect at least a fourth; but, thanks be to God, the doctors tell me this illness is not dangerous and is soon over. I am writing this to you therefore lest perhaps you should be deeply disturbed, hearing of my sickness from somebody else and thinking me to be more dangerously ill than I am. But commend me to the prayers of the sisters. Brother Henry from across the seas is restored to health as I hope, thanks to your prayers, and has already gone on before me into Germany. Take care then not to be frightened about my infirmity; for indeed I hope to gain by it both in body and in soul. The Lord gave us of his gifts both at Reggio and at Vercelli; and perhaps it was his good pleasure that, as was only just, I should not be given them entirely free. May his name be blessed for evermore,[14] Amen.

Farewell; and greet for me my beloved daughters and especially the prioress and Galiana and Cardiana and Juliet. Your brother and son, brother Gerard, sends tender greetings to you and to them. Let our brothers know of my condition, that they may pray for me, for I cannot write to them as time is so short.

May the Spirit of Christ Jesus be with your spirit, Amen.

---

[13] There was no priory at Vercelli.   [14] P. 71(72):17.

39

MILAN, SUMMER-AUTUMN 1231

To Diana, his beloved daughter in Christ Jesus, brother Jordan, useless servant of the Order of Preachers: healthy and the consolation of the Holy Spirit.

As I know you are anxious about me, I write to let you know that the Lord has hearkened to your prayers and those of your sisters: several days ago I began to get very much better, so much so that now I am almost, if not entirely, free of the fever which was vexing me and am well on the way to recovery though still very weak and exhausted. Give thanks then to the Lord who has thus begun to answer your prayers, and ask that if he so please, as he has begun so also he would finish his gracious task,[15] giving me greater strength and so restoring me swiftly to better health.

Greet and console my beloved daughters, your sisters, for me, and all those whom you know I would like to greet. Brother Gerard salutes you and them affectionately. Fare well in Christ Jesus, Amen.

40

(?) MILAN, SUMMER-AUTUMN 1231

To his beloved daughter in Christ Jesus, sister Diana, at Bologna, brother Jordan, useless servant of the Order of Preachers: health, and the consolation of the Paraclete.

I am not happy about what I hear of you, that you are so troubled and anxious about my illness. Would you have me taken from the number of the sons of God and be in no wise a sharer in the passion of our Redeemer Christ Jesus? Do you not know that the Lord scourgeth every son whom he receiveth?[16] And would you not have me received among

---

[15] *2 Cor* 8:6.   [16] *Heb* 12:6.

his sons? Is your zealous concern for me then truly worthy? If you would have me enter the kingdom you must suffer me to travel the road that leads to the kingdom, for through many tribulations we must enter there.[17] If this illness were to be to my hurt in any way then indeed I should be glad that you are distressed by it; but if it is good and fruitful for me, how could I want you, beloved, to be distressed by that good?

Wherefore if you wish me to be consoled, if you wish to remove the cause of my anxiety concerning you, cast out sadness from your own heart and be more readily consolable; simply commend me to the Lord and beg him that whatever pain the future may hold for me it may be turned into a means of my correction. The good and gentle Craftsman knows how greatly the clay for his handiwork stands in need of refining:[18] it is for us to submit ourselves in all things to his will, and leave all our ways in his hands.

But you must know that though latterly I was in grave danger, not only because of a quartan fever but on account of other maladies as well, now by the grace of God I am restored to health, and indeed one of the three fevers I had seems to have left no trace at all. Be comforted therefore; and keep before your mind the thought of that life which no infirmity can touch, as the prophet says: There shall no evil come to thee, nor shall the scourge come near thy dwelling.[19] Certainly here in the misery of our present sojourning the evils of sin come near to us; and since the sinner must again and again feel the lash[20] it is not surprising if here we are scourged for our wickedness. I am ready, then, for scourges,[21] if only I no evil of sin can enter there, can enter those serene and shining dwellings[22] into which may you and I together be gathered through the lovingkindness of him who is gentle and good, God's Son Jesus Christ who is blessed for ever and ever, Amen.

Farewell; salute my beloved daughters and comfort them in the Lord. Brother Gerard sends you and them his affectionate greetings.

---

[17] *Acts* 14:21.　　[18] Cp. *Rom* 9:21; *2 Tim* 2:20.　　[19] *Ps* 90(91):10.
[20] *Ps* 31(32):10.　　[21] *Ps* 37:18(38:17).　　[22] Cf. *supra*, p. 103, n. 4.

41

MILAN, SPRING 1232

To Diana, his beloved daughter in Jesus, brother Jordan, useless servant of the Order of Preachers: health, and the consolation of the Paraclete.

I know that you would have had me come to Bologna; and for me too it would have been a great consolation to have been able to do so; but in my present weak state the journey there and back would have been too much for me, and already it is high time for me to set out on the road to Paris for the General Chapter if, thanks to your prayers, the Lord will allow me to be present at it. Yet, though I do not at the present time come in the flesh to visit you, still I am with you in spirit; for wheresoever I go I yet remain with you, and though in the flesh you remain behind, in the spirit I carry you with me. As for my state of health, and the increase of strength which, thanks to your prayers, the Lord gives me daily, brother Nicholas the prior,[23] and the other brothers, will be able to give you full details if you ask them.

I must warn you, with regard to the little daughter of Lambertina, that if you should meet with any opposition to your wishes in this matter you must not let yourself be grievously distressed thereat but must bear all with patience, commending your cause to the Lord that he may vouchsafe to dispose and order this and all your affairs according to his good pleasure.[24] Only for the danger of losing God's grace should the souls of the saints[25] lament and be troubled; and even if the Lord were to permit this, still I would hope in his mercy that he would in other ways bestow on you yet greater abundance of his consolations; for we believe that no desolation is allowed to afflict the souls of the just in this life except for their good, so that, as the apostle says, to them that love God all things work together unto good, to such as according to his purpose are called to be saints.[26]

---

[23] Probably Nicholas Palea, prior provincial of the Roman province, who would return to Rome from Milan by way of Bologna.

[24] *Eph* 1:9.   [25] Cf. *supra*, p. 103, n. 4.   [26] *Rom* 8:24.

Greet for me all my beloved daughters in Christ Jesus, as also those others, outside the convent, to whom you know I would wish to send a spiritual greeting. May the grace and the bondage of Christ Jesus be with your spirit, beloved to me for ever, Amen.

42

TRENT, SUMMER 1232

To his beloved daughter in Christ, sister Diana of St. Agnes' in Bologna, brother Jordan, useless servant of the Order of Preachers: health, and the grace of spiritual joys.

After I had left Lombardy and had got as far as Trent on my way to Paris, I fell more seriously ill again, so that I was prevented from attending the General Chapter. And because of my absence it came about that the diffinitors, ill-informed about the state of affairs concerning St. Agnes,' made a regulation which would have been against your interests; but as soon as I heard of it, realizing that their decision had been a mistake, I rescinded it.

For your part, beloved, do not let yourself be distressed over such things: you have often had to bear with similar troubles in the past, and from their very recurrence you should by now be formed to patience. Am I not right? For though the Lord has sometimes allowed you to be afflicted for a space, yet has he always in his mercy delivered you, and will do so again and will help you to the end. Only cast your care upon him,[27] and put your affairs and those of the sisters in his hands, for he has care of you;[28] if sometimes he puts you to the test in this way it is that he may see how much thus far you have increased in strength and how much now you are able to bear for his sake.

As for my present state of health, you must know that I am once again much restored both in my body and in my head, so that I am able to preach to the students and the people, though I have not yet fully recovered all my former strength. I wrote recently to your prior provincial, telling him that I should be glad if he would grant the request of

[27] *Ps* 54:23 (55:22); *1 Pet* 5:7. [28] *1 Pet* 5:7.

brother Nicholas, the prior,[29] with regard to that girl;[30] do not be distressed at this: brother Nicholas was greatly concerned and made urgent
representations to me about the matter, and it seemed to me it would be
a great shame not to grant the request of such a man, so dear to us all
and so necessary to our Order. I beg you then to take this in good part.

43

(?), AUTUMN-WINTER 1232-33

*To Diana, his beloved daughter in Christ Jesus, brother Jordan,
useless servant of the Order of Preachers: health and joy in the Holy
Spirit.*

As I wish for strength and good health for myself, so do I for you too,
my beloved daughter, for my heart is one with your heart in the Lord;
rather, that part of myself which is yourself is by so much the better
part that I would much prefer to suffer anything burdensome myself
than allow it to fall upon you. Wherefore, beloved, strive always to
make progress, and to love God and cling to him with all your strength,
for it is good for you to cling to him and to put your trust in him;[31] say
therefore to him, My soul hath clung close to thee.[32]

For the rest, be of good heart, for soon by God's grace I shall see you
with my bodily eyes, you whom in spirit I never cease to see. Farewell,
and salute the sisters, my dearest daughters. Your son Gerard greets you
and them warmly. Beg them to pray for us till we arrive. May the Spirit
of the Lord Jesus be with your spirit, Amen. If you think you should
receive the daughter of Lambertina to the habit, you have my leave to
do so, and whatever steps you take in this matter, I approve them.

I, brother Gerard, your unworthy son, greet you, my dearest mother
and all my beloved sisters in Christ Jesus.

Greet for me all those whom I love and who love me, specially those
whom you know to be specially dear to me. Among all the cities of

---

[29] Cf. *Letter 41.*
[30] Presumably the "daughter of Lambertina" mentioned in *Letters 41* and *43.*
[31] *Ps* 72(73):28.   [32] *Ps* 62:9(63:8).

Lombardy, Tuscany, France, England, Provence and I might almost say Germany too, Bologna is something unique and very precious to me, the special possession[33] of my heart.

May the grace of Jesus Christ dwell in the depths of your soul, Amen.

44

PADUA, ADVENT 1232

To his beloved daughter Diana, brother Jordan, useless servant of the Order of Preachers, health and joy in the Holy Spirit.

Rejoice and be glad, O daughter of Sion[34] (though my beloved daughter also), rejoice, you and your sisters, and give thanks to our Lord Jesus, for behold your prayer has entered in to his sight[35] and gained his ear, and he has now given us many excellent and most suitable candidates from the schools at Padua and has touched the hearts of many more who still remain in the world and who therefore must be powerfully helped, now and henceforth, by your prayers, that the powerful bond which holds them back from their God may be broken. There is one in particular who is in great danger, so that he fears for his soul: for him especially I beg you to pray earnestly, that the Lord may not forsake him but may come to his aid and deliver him from all harm and adversity.

Do you also, beloved, be strengthened and consoled in the Lord,[36] and in the Child who is soon to be born for you: caress him, and tell him of your needs, for though he is small in body he is great and all-surpassing in his generosity and his mercy, blessed for ever, Amen.

Farewell in Christ. Greet for me all my daughters, your sisters, more especially the prioress, Galiana, Juliet and Cardiana.

---

33 *Ex.* 19:5; *Mal* 3:17.   34 *Zach(Zech)* 2:10; 9:9; *Soph(Zeph)* 3:14.
35 *Ps* 87:3(88:2).   36 *Eph* 7:10.

45

NORTHERN ITALY, PASSIONTIDE 1233

*To his beloved daughter in Jesus Christ, sister Diana of St. Agnes'
in Bologna, brother Jordan, useless servant of the Order of Preachers:
health, and the sweet blessings of the Spirit of knowledge.*[37]

Why, beloved daughter, do I write these poor little letters to you to
comfort your heart when you can find a far sweeter and more precious
consolation simply by taking up and reading that book which you have
daily before the eyes of your mind, the book of life, the book of the
Lord's perfect law which brings life back to souls?[38] This law, which is
called immaculate[39] because it takes away all stains, is charity: you see
it writ with wonderful beauty when you gaze on your Saviour Jesus
stretched out on the cross, as though a parchment, his wounds the writing, his blood the illuminations. Where, I ask you, my beloved, could
the lesson of love be learnt as it is learnt here? You know very well that
no letter can move the reader so vehemently to love as this.

On this then fix the keen gaze of your soul; hide yourself in the clefts
of this rock;[40] hide yourself away from the clamour of those who speak
wicked things.[41] Take up this book, open it and read, and you shall see
how the prophet finds in it lamentations and canticles and woe:[42]
lamentations for the sorrows which he bore; canticles for the joys which
he won for you by his sorrows; woe to eternal death from which by his
death he redeemed you.

From his lamentations learn to have patience within yourself; in his
canticles learn charity, for certainly you must love above all else him
who willed that you should be a partaker in joys so great; finally, when
you think that it is he who has snatched you from eternal woe, what
can you do but offer him thanksgiving and a song of praise?

See how I send you only this word writ very small;[43] yet to a loving
heart it will be long and deep enough. Do you then, my daughter, dwell
on it constantly and learn from it the wisdom of the saints, under the

[37] *Is* 11:2.   [38] *Ps* 18(19):8.   [39] Ibid.
[40] *Cant(Song)* 2:14.   [41] *Ps* 62:12(63:11).   [42] *Ezek* 2:9.
[43] Cf. *supra*, p. 95, n. 37.

tutorship and guidance and governance of God's Son Jesus Christ, to whom is honour and glory for ever and ever, Amen.[44]

Fare well in Christ Jesus. Salute for me those men and women whom you know I would like to greet. Brother Gerard, your son, salutes you. Pray for us, until we come.

46

(?), SPRING 1234 (?)

To his beloved daughter in Christ, sister Diana of St. Agnes' at Bologna, brother Jordan, useless servant of the Order of Preachers: eternal health.

Beloved, you know well in your wisdom how for as long as we are detained in the exile of this world we are all burdened by innumerable defects and cannot arrive at that stability which will be given us in the world to come, so that we fail to accept with equal mind all that befalls us, being sometimes too elated by good fortune, sometimes too much cast down by bad. It should not be so: since our desire is to attain to immortal life in the future we ought even now to conform ourselves in some measure to that future life, establishing our hearts in the strength of God and striving with all our might to fix on him all hope, all trust, all stability of purpose, so as to become like to him, who remains always firm and unmoved in himself. He is that secure refuge, never failing, always abiding, whereto the more we flee, the more steadfast we become in ourselves; whence it is that the saints, who had so great a trust in the Lord, were able so easily to make light of whatever misfortunes befell them.

Do you therefore, beloved, more and more flee to him; then, no matter what hardship or sorrow may befall you, your heart will be established upon so solid and firm a foundation that it will never be moved. Think often of this and impress it deeply upon your heart, and urge your sisters to do likewise.

I must add briefly for your consolation that I saw you recently in a dream: it seemed to me that you were speaking to me and in a manner so sincere and wise that still when I think of it I am filled with joy; and

---

[44] *Rom* 16:27.

you told me: The Lord spoke these words to me: I, Diana, I, Diana, I, Diana; and then added, the same number of times: Am good, am good, am good. I want you to know how consoling I found this.

47

STRASBOURG, AUGUST 1234

Brother Jordan, useless servant of the Order of Preachers, to his beloved daughter in Christ, sister Diana: may she be given joy heaped on joy and sweetness on sweetness in the Lord.

Your letter, beloved, brought me word—a good and delightful word, a word worthy of all welcome[45]—of the canonization of our holy father and of your joy in the Lord because of this; and I too rejoice, and I give thanks to God. I had not reached the end of the journey I had planned, since the messenger of the prior provincial caught up with me at Strasbourg on the vigil of the feast of St. Sixtus; and as we had already learnt of the canonization of our holy father from brother Raymond,[46] who is attached to the Roman curia, while the brethren at Strasbourg knew of it through a letter from brother Godfrey[47] who is also in the curia, we joyfully kept solemn festival together on the aforesaid vigil, to the honour of God and of our blessed father, giving thanks to the Son of God who is wonderful in his saints[48] and whose glory is seen in and through all things.

[45] *1 Tim* 4:9; St. Bernard of Clairvaux: *Sermo I in Vigil. Nativit. Domini.*

[46] [St. Raymond of Penyafort (1175–1275), who had been called to Rome by Gregory IX to collect and edit the vast collection of decrees and replies of the Roman Pontiffs over the centuries to simplify the work of canonist in the thirteenth century. The *Decretals of Gregory IX*, or the *Liber extra,* was promulgated on September 5, 1234. While other collections were compiled later that covered the years from 1234 on, the *Liber extra* remained a source of law for the Church (and a legal text for canonists) into the early twentieth century. With the promulgation of the first *Code of Canon Law* in 1917, the *Decretals* of Gregory IX ceased to have force, however, they served as part of the legal sources for this code. *Ed.*]

[47] Papal penitentiary; it was he who was later to write to the brethren in Paris to announce the death of Jordan.

[48] *Ps* 67:36(68:35).

Your poor foot, which I hear you have hurt, hurts me too; and makes me the more anxious that you should take more care not only of your foot but of your whole body.

Salute your sisters for me. I would have them, according to the exhortation of our holy father Augustine,[49] study tirelessly the commandments of the Lord and love them and effectively fulfil them, correcting through his grace whatever deviations therefrom they may find in themselves: let them hold fast to what is right, put away from them what is ugly, cultivate what is beautiful, preserve what is healthy, strengthen what is weak, and perseveringly keep to what is pleasing to God's Son, your Bridegroom, who is blessed for ever and ever, Amen.

48

PARIS, FEBRUARY-MARCH 1235

Brother Jordan, useless servant of the Order of Preachers, to sister Diana, bride of Christ Jesus and his own beloved daughter in the same: eternal health, and the consolations of the Holy Spirit.

The longer we are separated from one another, the greater becomes our desire to see one another again. Yet it is only by God's will (as I hope) that so far I have been prevented from coming to you; and if this was his will, it is for us to bend ours to conformity with it. All this winter since the Advent of the Lord I have been at Paris and by God's grace within this short space of time many excellent novices—men of high academic standing, Masters, and nobles, among them—have been given to us. When last I wrote to you the brethren were saying that already seventy-two had been received: for whom do you and your sisters give thanks to God. As far as my health is concerned, since I will soon be seeing you I will say now only that the fevers left me a long time ago but that I am having much trouble with one of my eyes and am in danger of losing it. Greet for me all my daughters in Christ and

---

[49] Called "father" in the Dominican Order inasmuch as the constitutional law of the Order is based on *The Rule of St. Augustine.* St. Dominic was himself an Augustinian canon before he set about his new work and the founding of the new Order.

commend me to them. Brother Gerard also sends you and them warm greetings. Farewell in Christ, Amen. Salute for me all those, men and women, who are dear to me in Christ.

49

PARIS (?), SUMMER 1235

To his beloved daughters in Jesus Christy the sisters of St. Agnes' in Bologna, brother Jordan, useless servant of the Order of Preachers: health, and the consolation of the Holy Spirit.

As you see, by God's will I have again been prevented from attending the General Chapter; and even had I no other cause for distress I should be sad simply because of you, because you above all I cannot see, nor find comfort in being with you. But we must bear with patience what our God ordains for us. In every possible way he makes plain to you how in this life we are not to fix our hopes on man nor seek our consolation in mortal things: he it is whom we are to love with our whole heart and our whole soul and our whole strength,[50] since only in him can we and ought we to find our sufficiency, in this life by his grace and in the life to come by his glory. In all things then, dear daughters, be constant and joyful and prudent, that you be counted not among the foolish virgins but among the wise.[51] I have not the time to write more to you now; but I commend you all, body and soul, to his mercy in whose hands are all the ends of the earth,[52] who is blessed for ever, Amen.

Fare you well, and pray for me. Gerard greets you devotedly and commends himself to your prayers.

---

[50] *Deut* 6:5; *Mt* 22:37.   [51] *Mt* 25:2 ff.   [52] *Ps* 94(95):4.

50

(?)1236

To his beloved daughter Diana in Bologna, brother Jordan, useless servant of the Order of Preachers: health, and the unfailing friendship of Jesus Christ.

Beloved, since I cannot see you with my bodily eyes nor be consoled with your presence as often as you would wish and I would wish, it is at least some refreshment to me, some appeasement of my heart's longing, when I can visit you by means of my letters and tell you how things are with me, just as I long to know how things are with you, for your progress and your gaiety of heart are a sweet nourishment to my soul—though you for your part do not know to what ends of the earth I may be journeying and even if you knew you would not have messengers to hand by whom you could send something to me. Yet whatever we may write to each other matters little, beloved: within our hearts is the ardour of our love in the Lord whereby you speak to me and I to you continuously in those wordless outpourings of charity which no tongue can express nor letter contain.[53]

O Diana, how unhappy this present condition of things which we must suffer: that we cannot love each other without pain and anxiety! You weep and are in bitter grief because it is not given you to see me continually; and I equally grieve that it is so rarely given me to be with you. Who shall bring us into the strong city,[54] into the city of the Lord of Hosts[55] that the Highest himself hath founded,[56] where we shall no more have to long either for him or for one another? Here on earth we are wounded every day and our hearts are torn to shreds; and every day our miseries cause us to cry out, Who shall deliver us from the body of this death?[57]

But no: these things we must bear with patience and, so far as our daily work allows, dwell in mind and heart with him who alone can deliver us from our distresses,[58] in whom alone is rest, apart from

---

[53] Cf. the hymn, *Jesu dulcis memoria* [attributed to St. Bernard of Clairvaux. *Ed.*]
[54] *Ps* 59:11(60:9).   [55] *Ps* 47:9(48:8).   [56] *Ps* 86(87):5.   [57] *Rom* 8:24.
[58] *Ps* 24(25):17.

whom we shall find nothing but misery and abundance of sorrow wheresoever we look. Meanwhile then let us accept with joy whatever sad things may come to us; for with what measure our trials are meted to us, so shall be measured our joy,[59] poured out on us by God's Son Jesus Christ, to whom is honour and glory and strength and empire for ever and ever, Amen.[60]

Pray for me, as indeed I know you do; and greet for me the prioress and Galiana; greet each and all of our friends outside the convent and yet more specially those who are in the house with you, if they should come to see you,[61] and commend me to their prayers. Farewell, beloved daughter, in God's Son Jesus Christ.

---

[59] Cp. *Mt* 7:2.   [60] *Apoc(Rev)* 7:12; *1 Tim* 6:16.
[61] This would refer to the *conversae* or *familiares*; cf. *supra*, Letter 8, p. 60, n. 62.

APPENDIX
Other Letters

Other Letters

THE following six letters are added here, though they were not written to Diana, partly because of their relevance to matters mentioned in some of the letters to her but mainly because of the further light they throw both on Jordan's personality and on his teaching. The first shows how, when occasion demanded, he could be not only firm in action but also astringently tart in expression; the next two reveal the strength of his feeling for Henry of Cologne more fully than the short *Letter 17* to Diana: these, and the fourth and perhaps the fifth also, were written to a Benedictine nun of the abbey of Trèves who may have been related to Henry and in any case must have known and loved him well since Jordan refers to him here as *dilectus noster,* beloved to both of them.

1

Brother Jordan, useless servant of the Order of Preachers, to his beloved son in Christ, brother Stephen, prior provincial of Lombardy: eternal health.

Your conscience has evidently been startled and affrighted at a mere rustle of leaves, since you imagine that the Constitution forbidding the brethren to admit women to the habit, the tonsure and the taking of vows, was directed against the sisters of St. Agnes':[1] in thinking thus you have given credence to the spirit of some who in this respect are not of God,[2] and thereby have pointlessly made difficulties for yourself. Such an idea never entered the heads of any of the diffinitors: they were concerned solely with those brothers who, in some of our provinces such as Germany and elsewhere, had become accustomed on their preaching-missions to receive too readily to the habit, tonsure and vows, either penitent harlots wishing to live a life of penance or young girls wishing to take a vow of chastity.

---

[1] Cf. *supra, Letter 29.*   [2] *1 Jn* 4:1.

I know fully all the acts and decrees of all the Chapters, and the intentions of those who made the decrees; and I know that when this present law was passed the idea that it should refer to our own sisters was not only never raised, it was never even thought of. For indeed this would have meant their being completely cut off from us. And even if this had been our intention, would it have lain within our power? Most certainly not: it would have meant a defiance of the Pope, by whose command we are charged with the care of them just as much as of the brethren. Let there be no further uncertainty in your mind, then, about this; and do not, by discussing it with others, raise any doubts about what ought to be perfectly clear and straightforward.

As for other matters: if anyone supposes that I have not the power of dispensation with regard to Order regulations, that seems to me the same as saying that the office of Master General was never committed to me. Nothing in the Constitutions, however grave, is to be regarded as being beyond my power to dispense with if I think fit to do so in view of special needs of times, places or persons, except for the three laws which, at the last Chapter at Paris,[3] were so firmly established as not to allow of either revocation or dispensation, and which indeed we thought of asking the Curia to confirm. That everything else is within my power to dispense with I have no doubt whatever, such as for instance giving leave to journey on horseback, to take money with one, and other things of that or of other kinds whether great or small; if it were otherwise how could I have dared to assume to myself a power I had in no wise received? No, in this respect I have by God's grace nothing with which to reproach myself: in all the dispensations I have granted up till now I have unquestionably been within my rights.

Wherefore, beloved son, put aside all scrupulosity in this matter, and instead learn for the future to be more solidly convinced than before of the folly of changing one's views each time one hears a fresh opinion put forward. You must also assure the sisters of St. Agnes' that they have nothing to fear from this law, and so restore to them a sense of complete security, that they may persevere in peace in the name of the Lord.

I write to you from Genoa, in good health and ready to set sail for Montpellier. I wrote just recently, I think, to the prior of Bologna about the harvest which the Lord gave us in Vercelli; but since you ask me

---

[3] The *Capitulum Generalissimum* (General Chapter) of 1228.

about it I will recount it again. At first I found the scholars there extremely unreceptive, and I was on the point of saying my farewells and departing when suddenly the generous hand of the Lord brought to us Master Walter of Germany, the regent of logic, a past master in his art who at Paris had been regarded as among the greatest of the Masters, and he was followed by his two best Bachelors, one a Provençal, the other a Lombard, both of them ready, had I wished it, for the work of teaching; then came an excellent German student of canon law, a canon of Spires and rector of the German students at Vercelli; and another German, Master Gotteschalk, canon of Maastricht, a most learned and distinguished man; then finally two excellent men from Provence joined us, both members of the faculty of law, the one lecturing on canon, and the other on civil, law. It might almost have seemed as though we had picked all these out specially from the entire university. Yet more followed, also men of distinction, so that altogether twelve or thirteen entered in a very short space of time. I brought nearly all of them with me to Genoa; two went straight on to Montpellier, the rest will stay on here for a time; five of them are Lombards. For all this we must give thanks to God, who pours out his blessings so continually upon us and upon our children.[4]

Farewell in the Lord, and pray for me. Greet the brethren and our other friends for me, and commend me to their prayers. Among the novices remaining at Genoa is one from Cremona named Peregrinus, a man of very good repute, well-versed in logic and, they say, of noble birth; he is likely to make excellent progress: after he has been here some time you will be able to move him to whatever convent of the province you think best from the point of view of studies.

2

To the beloved bride of Christ Jesus at St. Oeren, brother Jordan, useless servant of the Order of Preachers: eternal health.

Since God shall wipe away all tears from the eyes of the saints,[5] he must surely wipe away those which you shed so abundantly as I left you; and

---

[4] *Ps* 113:22(115:14).   [5] *Apoc(Rev)* 21:4.

I had indeed hoped that with the inspiration of the Paraclete, the gentle Comforter, I might send back to you by letter some small consolation. But alas, alas, alas, my hope is made void; all consolation is hidden from my eyes: he who divides to every one according as he will,[6] will not now make a separation between beloved brothers,[7] for according to his good pleasure he has already done so. Wherefore I weep, I weep for my sweetest friend, my dearest brother, my most beloved son, Henry, the prior of Cologne. He, dearest sister, he, before Advent, at Cologne, left this life to go to the Lord: he (how happy!) happily went on his way, and me (how unhappy!) he left, to remain unhappily in this present wicked world.[8]

Who now shall take his place in summoning men to the citadel of Sion, now that he, the angel of peace, who brought peace and light to his fatherland, has gone to his eternal fatherland? Nor without reason do I call him an angel, he who lived, in this world, an angelic life. He was indeed a messenger of the Lord of Hosts, speaking with the tongues of angels rather than of men, not a sounding brass, a tinkling cymbal,[9] but a cymbal of joy, praising and preaching the Lord with his whole spirit.[10] He was beloved by all his brethren, both because he was more beloved of God than all his brethren and because he was himself a lover of the brethren, as also of the people of Israel,[11] which is to say all the faithful who set the Lord always in their sight.[12]

O my brother Jonathan, so well beloved![13] You were a gift to me from the glorious dove,[14] the Virgin Mary. When I had determined in my heart to enter the Order I asked my Lady to give him to me as a brother; and this she did, in virtue not of my prayers but of her loving mercy. And he for his part begged of my Lady, with many tears, to give him the will to enter the Order with me: he begged, and obtained: the dove, the chosen one of God gave him to the Order, and being the dove's gift he himself walked in the simplicity of the dove and therefore with confidence. He was a good labourer in the Lord's vineyard; and he was called by the Lord, not when evening was come, but already at the sixth hour, and received his wage:[15] he ran, not with the slowness of old age but with the swiftness and ardour of youth in flower, and so,

---

[6] *1 Cor* 12:11.   [7] *Osee (Hos)* 13:15.   [8] *Gal* 1:4.   [9] *1 Cor* 13:1.
[10] *Ps* 150:5.   [11] *2 Mack (Macc)* 15:14.   [12] *Ps* 15(16):8.
[13] *2 Kings (2 Sam)* 1:26.   [14] *Cant (Song)* 6:8.   [15] *Mt* 20:5 ff.

outrunning others,[16] obtained the sooner the heavenly prize, the incorruptible crown.[17] O good and faithful servant,[18] who for the talent which the Lord gave you gained others over and above[19] and so, your duty faithfully performed, have entered, freed of all care for evermore, into the joy of your beloved Lord! Now that death has taken you I praise you; now that all is consummated for you I preach your greatness.

See, beloved, how against all my hope and expectation God has done this to me: and what consolation can you look for from me now in my desolation? But the blessed God, Jesus Christ, whose name I send you by the hand of my son Felix, he, who comforteth the humble,[20] will also comfort both you and me; and as on the cross he committed his mother to the care of his disciple,[21] so may he now, in all your sorrow, enfold you in the care of his grace.

3

To the virgin-bride of Christ, well-beloved in Christ and dwelling close to my heart like the cluster of myrrh, even though dwelling in the Storehouse[22] of the glorious Virgin Mary: a cluster of myrrh not only inasmuch as stored away in the storehouse, but as sifted and refined by trial and temptation,[23] as prepared in the fire of fervent meditation in Christ, as set upon the table like the loaves of proposition[24] hot from the oven, as renewed every sabbath[25] through the glad contemplation of Christ whom you desire: whom also, having long desired, may you at length wholly possess.

This is a long salutation with which to greet you, beloved sister, or if you will permit me so to call you, daughter: rather let me say both sister and daughter; but however long a salutation may be it cannot adequately express even a small affection, and what then shall I say of that

---

[16] *Jn* 20:4.   [17] *1 Cor* 9:24.   [18] *Mt* 25:21.

[19] *Mt* 25:20.   [20] *2 Cor* 7:6.   [21] *Jn* 19:26.

[22] A play on the name of the abbey: in German, St. Oeren; in Latin, "*Horreum*" a storehouse.

[23] The Latin is "*in arca excutitur per tentationes.*"

[24] *Ex* 25:30.   [25] *Lev* 24:8.

very great charity wherewith I greatly love you in Jesus our Mediator, who makes a unity not only in mankind, of those who love one another in Christ, but between mankind and God,[26] since he hath made both one:[27] for at one and the same time he brought it about that God should be man and man should be God, and that man should love God in man and man in God. Beloved and ever to be loved is this love, in which he enfolds not only the angels but also the sons of Abraham. Let us then love one another[28] in him and through him and for him; and in that same love for one another let us so run, led by him who is the way and who is the truth,[29] that in the end we may by his bounty come to him who is also the life[30] and who lives and reigns in the life and kingdom of glory.

I would be instructed, and indeed compelled, by love itself to write more to you of love, but now in truth I cannot, for our beloved has gone from us, has gone far away from us,[31] the blossom has withered and our vines shall yield no longer their sweet smell[32] but now only bitterness; no longer is the voice of the turtle-dove heard in our land: arise then, make haste, and weep for the flower that is withered, the dove that is heard no more.[33] You know of whom I speak: of Henry, your Henry, or rather mine; better, both yours and mine, mine and yours, beloved to us both, or more rightly still, beloved of all since he was all things to all men that he might save all.[34]

Among all flowers he will be likened especially to the lily and the rose. Rightly will he be likened to the lily, for the candour of his innocence shone bright and white like the lily: to this I testify, and I know that my testimony is true,[35] for to me it was given, though unworthy, to cull the last flowers from his heart's garden, and there I found a spotless purity of heart and body alike which he had zealously sought from his early youth and kept unsullied till his death. But I also found there in bloom the rose of charity; and of the fragrance of these flowers it was not I alone who was aware but the whole province, running thereafter[36] with loins girt to obtain the prize.[37]

---

[26] *1 Tim* 2:5.   [27] *Eph* 2:14.   [28] *1 Jn* 4:7.   [29] *Jn* 14:6.
[30] Ibid.   [31] *"abiit et recessit"*: cp. *Cant (Song)* 2:11.
[32] *Cant(Song)* 2:13.   [33] *Cant(Song)* 2:10-12.   [34] *1 Cor* 9:22.
[35] *Jn* 19:35.   [36] *Cant(Song)* 1:3.   [37] *1 Cor* 9:24.

Weep then with me, as I lament him for whom the whole of Cologne and indeed of Germany is weeping. True, we are not to be sorrowful even as those others who have no hope;[38] yet I confess to you, I think I have never wept so much for the death of anyone. I wept before he died, I wept as he died, I wept after he had died. Yet I wept gladly; my tears were tears not of desolation but of consolation; the tears not of one bewailing and lamenting the dead but of one praying with devoted mind to the living God, as is sometimes the case with devout people when a church keeps the festival of its holy patrons. And in fact the feast day of the blessed Severinus, archbishop of Cologne, was his birthday in the Lord, the day when he went forth from this life and, being dead to the world, was born to God, to Christ.

This was on the night of the ninth day before the Kalends of November:[39] the bell had rung for Matins, and I went to see him before going to the choir. I found him breathing with difficulty, on the point of entering into his agony; I asked him if he wished to receive the last anointing. He replied that he did indeed so wish, and begged that we should fulfil his desire before beginning the Office. So it was done. He seemed rather to be giving than receiving the anointing, so devoutly did he recite the prayers. Thereafter we went into Matins, and celebrated the Office of the blessed Severinus with its nine lessons; and as I listened to these and the chant too, my heart applied them to him who was still on his way home, to Henry; I sighed for grief, and tears flooded over me unrestrained;[40] then they began to flow yet more copiously but sweetly.

So, having gone back to him, I found him speaking ardently of God and with God, singing, and inflaming himself and those around him with desire for our heavenly home, deploring this our present exile yet consoling his brethren and crying to them: My brothers, my heart yearns for you. As he said this he began to exult in spirit and to sing joyously again and again: Blessed Virgin, pray that we may be made worthy of the heavenly bread; and then to those already shining as lights in the world, as stars in the firmament,[41] he cried: The Lord hath chosen you for his own possession.[42]

These and many other like things he said, expressing his own longing for death and exhorting us to goodness of life; then, preparing his

---

[38] *1 Thess* 4:12. [39] i.e. October 23. [40] *Job* 3:24.
[41] *Gen* 1:16-17. [42] *Ps* 134(135):4.

blessed soul, as the Lord called him and as that enemy who lies in wait for every heel[43] was powerless against him, he spoke the word of Jacob: If God shall be with me, and shall keep me in the way by which I walk, and shall give me bread to eat and raiment to put on, the Lord shall be my God,[44] and Christ's cross shall be as a stone for a monument.[45]

Then, after he had spoken a little longer, he said: The prince of this world cometh, and in me he hath not anything;[46] and thereafter added a number of other sayings worthy of memory; then he entered into his agony while we, weeping and lamenting, commended his soul to God, our prayers interrupted sometimes by silence, sometimes by sobs. And then what tears, what lamentings,[47] when not only did so good a father leave the sons he loved so well, and they were deprived of their father, but I also, his father however unworthily, lost a son of whom I had so great a need! Without anguish I had begotten him, but not without anguish did I lose him; and yet I have not lost him, I have but sent him on before me, he who while still in his youth yet full of days[48] did not die but rather fell asleep in the Lord.[49] This thought is even more of a consolation to me than his absence is a desolation: may you be consoled by it also. You have in him a faithful messenger and intercessor with Christ: pray for him to the Lord, that he being thereby the more swiftly purified may, dwelling in perfect purity with God, pray for you.

Commend him to the prayers of others. Pray also for me, as I often do for you. Farewell in Christ Jesus.

4

Brother Jordan, unprofitable servant of the Order of Preachers, to my beloved daughter in Christ at St. Oeren: may you follow the Lamb without spot whithersoever he goeth.[50]

From the day when you proposed in your mind to seek and search out[51] how you should leave wholly behind you not only your kinsfolk and

---

[43] *Gen* 3:15.   [44] *Gen* 28:20-21.   [45] *Gen* 28:22.   [46] *Jn* 14:30.

[47] Perhaps an echo of the *Benedictus* antiphon of the feast of St. Martin of Tours: "*O quantus erat luctus omnium, quanta praecipue maerentium lamenta monachorum!*" (Roman Breviary).

[48] *Gen* 25:8.   [49] *Acts* 7:59.   [50] *Apoc(Rev)* 14:4.   [51] *Eccl* 1:13.

possessions but even your own self you became most lovable to the Lord. Stand therefore, beloved, like an immovable column in the fear of God and in the rule of your Order; and school yourself to piety, which is the honouring of God; for piety, as the apostle says, is profitable to all things.[52] Withdraw yourself so far as may be from idle gossipings and confabulations; unite yourself to God in the assiduous intimacy of prayer; may the beloved Jesus be your bridegroom, and the face of your beloved, chosen out of thousands,[53] be your delight: your beloved, white and ruddy[54] surrounded by the red blossoms of roses and the white lilies of the valleys, the choirs of martyrs and virgins, he himself both virgin and martyr. In him seek and find your true friend; and to him commend me also, a sinner, as I rely upon you to do. Fare you well.

5

Brother Jordan, useless servant of the Order of Preachers, to the chosen bride of Christ Jesus: salvation from our God;[55] and the word in your heart: I am here to save you.[56]

The love wherewith according to God's will you sincerely and fervently enfold me in Christ brings to your mind the one thought concerning me: that I love you in return. And so indeed I do; else I would not be an imitator of him who says, I love them that love me.[57] For this even the heathen and the publicans do,[58] so that did I not love you I should be worse than they.

Yet I know that it is you who love the more; and it grieves me that your love should thus be cheated. I wrong you: for a long time now you have been sowing in my soul's barren soil the seed of your love, and you do not reap what you have sown: you have sowed much and brought in little:[59] the love you reap is much less than that which you have poured out for me in such abundance.

But suffer it patiently:[60] it is not to you alone that I do this wrong, but to your bridegroom Christ, whose Father the Husbandman has now for a long time been waiting to receive from me precious fruit[61]

---

[52] *1 Tim* 4:8. [53] *Cant(Song)* 5:10. [54] Ibid. [55] *Ps* 97(98):3.
[56] *Ps* 34(35):3. [57] *Prov* 8:17. [58] *Mt* 5:46. [59] *Aggeus(Hag)* 1:6.
[60] *1 Pet* 2:20. [61] *Jas* 5:7.

from his precious seed: for God so loved me as to give his only-begotten Son for me.[62] How true the love, how good the seed, that I have received from him! Yet where is the fruit? Where even a small return for a love so great? For if, Lord, you are Father also, where is the love that is your due?[63] O accursed earth of mine, bringing forth thorns and thistles![64]

This then, if you consider, must surely be enough for the handmaid, that she be as her Lord.[65] I rejoice that I am loved by you; but my joy is the less because you are less loved by me. You love fully and utterly because you think that through me you received the gift of conversion and the words of life; but I think that we had not yet come together when you were found to be with child of the Holy Spirit;[66] wherefore your love for me is all the more gratuitous, just as the confidence you repose in me in wanting to rely on my counsel is all the more abundant. But may the Angel of Great Counsel bestow on us his good counsel and his good pleasure.

I know that you long to go forth out of your country and from your kindred;[67] but this longing I would not at the present time dare to encourage, nor must you think of yourself as being among those inhabitants of the earth unto whom the devil is come down and to whom is woe.[68] The devil has not descended to you; rather have you ascended on high[69] to Christ, in clinging to whom is all your content,[70] as you find in heaven your true home.[71] If this should not seem true to you, remember that for the love of God you are become a stranger and a sojourner upon the earth,[72] and all the more a sojourner in that your friends and neighbours are before your eyes. But the day will come when you shall no longer be a sojourner upon the earth but shall have everlasting gladness with the angels in heaven, exulting and rejoicing in the choir of virgins who sing a new song which none but they can sing, being without spot before the throne of God and following the spotless Lamb whithersoever he goeth.[73]

This joy shall you have as you gaze at him in his splendour on whom the angels desire to look[74] and at whose beauty sun and moon

---

[62] *Jn* 3:16. [63] Cp. *Mal* 1:6. [64] *Gen* 3:18. [65] *Mt* 5:25.
[66] *Mt* 1:18. [67] *Gen* 12:1. [68] *Apoc(Rev)* 12:12; 8:13.
[69] *Eph* 4:8. [70] *Ps* 72(73):28. [71] *Phil* 3:20. [72] *Ps* 38:13(39:12).
[73] *Apoc(Rev)* 14:3-5. [74] *1 Pet* 1:12.

are filled with wonder, while you for your part will be surrounded with the waving and glistering blossoms of spring.[75] Then like Job shall you forget misery,[76] and the former things which shall have passed away shall no longer be held in your memory for God will wipe away every tear from your eyes.[77]

Why then are you consumed with grief? Is your counsellor perished?[78] On the contrary, hearken to what this divine counsellor tells you: Thus said the daughter of Sion, The Lord hath forsaken me and the Lord hath forgotten me. But can a woman forget her infant, so as not to have pity on the son of her womb? and if she should forget, yet will not I forget thee; behold, I have graven thy image in the palms of my hands.[79] This word he says through the prophet Isaiah, and his word is true. If then he should sometimes withdraw himself from you for a little while, yet again a little while and you shall see him again.[80] This little while may indeed seem long to you; if yet he tarry[81] await him, for he that is to come will come and will not delay;[82] and he will console you, he that comforteth the humble,[83] Jesus Christ who is blessed for ever, Amen.[84]

6

Brother Jordan, useless servant of the Order of Preachers, to his beloved sons in the Son of God, the prior and community at Paris: health, and the grace to dwell in mind in the things that are above, not the things that are of earth.[85]

I have heard, beloved sons, and had great joy and gladness in the hearing,[86] of how you dwell in perfect unity in the house,[87] and that you are instant in prayer,[88] diligent in study, and growing in peace and mutual charity among yourselves;[89] wherefore my soul must needs rejoice and

---

[75] Antiphon viii & Responsory ii for Matins of St. Agnes, [Emmanuel Suarez, O.P, Ed. *Breviarium juxta ritum S. Ordinis Praedicatorum*, (Rome, Santa Sabina, 1952). *Ed.*]

[76] *Job* 11:16.   [77] *Apoc(Rev)* 21:4.   [78] *Mic* 4:9.

[79] *Is* 49:15.   [80] *Jn* 26:17.   [81] *Mt* 25:5.

[82] *Heb* 10:37.   [83] *2 Cor* 7:6.   [84] *2 Cor* 11:31.

[85] *Col* 3:2.   [86] *Ps* 50:10(51:8).   [87] *Rule of St. Augustine.*

[88] *Rom* 12:12.   [89] *1 Pet* 4:8.

praise and bless the Lord, and all that is within me must bless his holy name.[90] In these days of joy and solemn festival I consider how Christ, our life and resurrection,[91] rising again from the dead dieth now no more;[92] and it seems to me that you are among those whose bodies rose with Christ in witness of his resurrection.[93]

I would not flatter you, nor, I hope, does any among you flatter himself, though indeed it is proper for all those to rejoice and to glory in the Lord[94] who are conscious of having trampled under foot the former death of sin and of walking now in newness of life,[95] and who moreover refuse to make a pact with death, rising like Lazarus only to die again, but instead, having within them the seeds of immortal life, labour day by day that the spirit of their minds be again and again renewed.[96]

We have trust then in the Lord[97] who hath called us out of the darkness of death into the marvellous light of this resurrection[98] in which you stand, that you seek nothing else but this. Behold, you are risen together with Christ and from henceforth you must in no wise understand as children:[99] you must understand the things that are above, where Christ sitteth at the right hand of God.[100] Pray, toil, press on: that for such time as it is not yet given you to see Jesus in the heavenly Galilee,[101] he may yet visit you wheresoever you may be and may show himself to you as before he showed himself to his disciples, showing by many proofs that he was still alive, for forty days appearing to them and speaking of the kingdom of God[102] and so at sundry times and in divers manners[103] most generously consoled them.

If there should be among you anyone who, like Mary, having tears for his portion,[104] should first have worthily washed his feet with them,[105] he will not be deprived of the consolation of seeing him if, coming early, he stands at the sepulchre, weeping.[106] Nor shall a Peter not forthwith have sight of him if, having denied Jesus, he repent and weep bitterly[107] over his denial. And if there be some who have learnt fully by experience in their own lives the truth of the saying that while we are in

90 *Ps* 102(103):1   91 *Jn* 11:25.   92 *Rom* 6:9.

93 *Mt* 27:52.   94 *2 Cor* 10:17   95 *Rom* 6:4.

96 *2 Cor* 4:16; *Eph* 4:23.   97 *Phil* 2:24.   98 *1 Pet* 2:9.

99 *1 Cor* 13:11.   100 *Col* 3:1.   101 *Mt* 28:7.

102 *Acts* 1:3.   103 *Heb* 1:1.   104 *Ps* 79:6(80:5).

105 *Lk* 7:44.   106 *Jn* 20:1, 11.   107 *Lk* 22:62.

the body we are absent from the Lord,[108] and who, pitying themselves because their sojourning is prolonged,[109] make their way sorrowfully, as though exiled from Jerusalem, to the village of Emmaus,[110] truly they also shall in some measure have sight of Jesus, so that as the fire of devotion begins to burn fiercely within them they ask with wonder: Was not our heart burning within us whilst he spoke to us in the way?[111]

It remains, beloved sons, that before all these things you must have a constant mutual charity among yourselves,[112] for it cannot be that Jesus will appear to those who have cut themselves off from the unity of the brotherhood: Thomas, for not being with the other disciples when Jesus came,[113] was denied sight of him: and will you think yourself more holy than Thomas? Wherefore I declare to the sensual man who has not the Spirit,[114] who prefers his own private interests to the common good,[115] who walks according to his own selfish desires: that he will not see Jesus unless he has more zeal for that charity which seeketh not her own,[116] which knows nothing of divisions and dissensions but rejoices in the common good and loves the unity of the brotherhood. Such a man may from time to time feel some very slight and fugitive consolation of spirit: he can never fully have sight of the Lord unless he is with the disciples gathered together in the house.[117]

These ideas I wished to commend to you, beloved sons, since we are keeping the season of Easter, in the hope that you are indeed already carrying them out faithfully but that you will seek to do so yet more perfectly, being consoled and guided in all things by God's Son Jesus Christ, to whom is honour and empire everlasting, Amen.

---

[108] *2 Cor* 5:6.
[109] *Ps* 119(120):5.
[110] *Lk* 24:17.
[111] *Lk* 24:32.
[112] *1 Pet* 4:8.
[113] *Jn* 20:24.
[114] *Jude* 19; *1 Cor* 2:14.
[115] Cf. *Rule of St. Augustine*.
[116] *1 Cor* 13:5.
[117] *Jn* 20:19.

EDITOR'S AFTERWORD

Jordan's letters to Diana still inspire and encourage "his beloved daughters in Christ,"[1] the Dominican nuns of today, who continue to share in the universal preaching mission of the Dominican Order through their life of contemplation, liturgical prayer, study, work, and sacrifice. From the small beginnings of the first nine nuns at Prouilhe, France, in 1206, there are now around 3,500 nuns in 234 monasteries throughout the world.

"The vocation of the nuns places them at the heart of the Order. Such was the desire of St. Dominic in order to emphasize in a radical way the grace of contemplation, which is the very source of the itinerant apostolic life begun by him. In solidarity with the mission of their preaching brothers as well as that of the whole Dominican family, the nuns, by their prayer, accompany 'the Word which does not return to God without accomplishing that for which it was sent.' This contemplation takes root both in silence and liturgical prayer, in the day-to-day of life lived in common, but also in meditation and assiduous study of the word of God, informed and inspired by the theological and spiritual masters."[2]

Essentially a mystery, their life is a collective, sacred sign and witness of Gospel living and an anticipation of the glorious Church without spot or wrinkle and immutable in its possession and contemplation of God. Theirs is a lifestyle radically lived for the sake of the Kingdom of Heaven: a way of living that witnesses to, proclaims, and serves the coming of God's own rule of peace, justice, mercy and love initiated by Christ the Lord, and completed on His return.

The specific mission of the Dominican nuns is unceasing prayer for the entire Church, and particularly for the Order. It is a pure, spiritual service in the form of praise, adoration, intercession, expiation and thanksgiving. By profession, the nuns are wholly consecrated to the

---

[1] A favorite salutation used by Jordan in his letters to Diana and her sisters at the Monastery of St. Agnes, Bologna.

[2] André Duval. *Dominicaines moniales de l'Ordre des Prêcheurs*. (Paris: C.I.F. Éditions, 1993).

Church and are called to the task of spreading the Kingdom of God in the world, using the means of prayer and penance, which nevertheless are endowed with marvelous apostolic fruitfulness. The nuns harbor in their hearts the sufferings and anguish of all; they share to a more universal degree the fatigue and hope of all people; they raise the level of the spiritual life of the Church and are a sign to believers and unbelievers of the existence and presence of God, affirming the transcendent values of the life to come. "By their hidden life, they proclaim prophetically that in Christ alone is true happiness to be found, here by grace and afterwards by glory."[3]

For more information on the Dominican contemplative life, please visit the Order's website at www.op.org/international/english/Nuns/directory.htm.[4]

---

[3] Fundamental Constitutions of the Nuns V, (*Book of Constitutions of the Nuns of the Order of Preachers*, 1987), p. 30.

[4] Most of the content of this afterward has been adapted from the pamphlet of Mother Marie Rosaria Hiett, O.P., "Those Mysterious Nuns," (Summit, NJ: Dominican Nuns, [1970]).

NOTE

The following list is appended for readers who may wish to refer to the Latin text of the Letters in the Altaner edition, since the order in which they are given there is quite different from that of the Aron translation which has been followed here.

Letter 1 here is Letter 51 in Altaner
2	35
3	19
4	20
5	21
6	38
7	17
8	34
9	40
10	27
11	24
12	30
13	31
14	45
15	33
16	22
17	44
18	32
19	18
20	28
21	8
22	23
23	29
24	39
25	12
26	25
27	1

28	14
29	48
30	10
31	41
32	16
33	11
34	26
35	46
36	36
37	4
38	7
39	6
40	3
41	2
42	47
43	5
44	50
45	15
46	9
47	43
48	42
49	37
50	13

In the Appendix of this present book:

Letter 1 is Letter	49 in Altaner
2	53
3	52
4	54
5	55
6	56

978-0-595-38586-7
0-595-38586-9

Printed in the USA
CPSIA information can be obtained
at www.ICGtesting.com
LVHW041128081023
760496LV00005B/169